PRAISE FOR MEGAN STIELSTRA

"Holy shit. I read *Once I Was Cool* in two and a half hours, then I started reading it again."

—JAMIE IREDELL, AUTHOR OF *I WAS A FAT DRUNK CATHOLIC SCHOOL INSOMNIAC*

"Megan Stielstra's voice is so palpable, so immediate and vibrantly alive, it feels as though she's standing right in front of you, sashaying her hips a little and maybe occasionally breaking into song, making you laugh so hard you don't quite notice when you start to cry. A trickster constantly unpacking and upending what is meant by "fiction," "truth" and "storytelling," Stielstra has ultimately created a charming style wholly her own."

—GINA FRANGELLO, AUTHOR OF *A LIFE IN MEN*

"Here's the thing about Megan Stielstra: she has a profound understanding of where we all go in our minds, and the unique ability to turn it into a story that sounds like your new best friend is telling it to you. You know, the kind where you're going "Oh my god that totally happened to me" or "It's like you see inside my head" until she gets to the part where there's suddenly a marching band following her down the street or she's sleeping with the Incredible Hulk or having a three-way which is the part where you go "Okay that didn't happen to me but damn, why does it still seem like it did?" Megan Stielstra brings it to the party and rocks it."

—ELIZABETH CRANE, AUTHOR OF *WE ONLY KNOW SO MUCH*

D0596079

"*Everyone Remain Calm* is a rarity: a bold, imaginative, and cunning collection of stories. Spanning a wide variety of styles, forms, and tones, the language here is unapologetically inventive and often humorous, while the sentiments are deeply heartfelt. Ms. Stielstra's inimitable voice is a fiercely unique creation."

—JOE MENO, AUTHOR OF *THE GREAT PERHAPS*

"Stielstra—collector, curator and facilitator of so many stories—also writes beautifully and kinetically. Her work possesses a rare aural quality, no doubt the result of so much time on stage, or even in front of a classroom... in *Everyone Remain Calm* she gleefully tests the boundaries of the short-story form."

—*TIME OUT CHICAGO*

"Stielstra has staked her career on live performance storytelling that is often emulated but never duplicated. In print and especially live, she urges the audience to come with her on adventures that can get both hysteric in pitch and absolutely still: few performers can teeter their audience between these extremes while still engaging such a personal connection. It is the story that reigns supreme, that dictates what will happen on stage. Her delivery is just one part of the show, like the musicians that back her, or the singer that swaps a story duet, or the brass band parading around her." —*CHICAGO LITERARY EXAMINER*

"Her theatrical performances are intense, composed of a powerful cadence of speech and strong storytelling you won't find anywhere else. Somehow she has bottled the presence of her performances and sprinkled a little bit on each story contained within *Everyone Remain Calm.*" —*CBS CHICAGO, BEST NEW CHICAGO BOOKS*

Megan Stielstra

PERSONAL ESSAYS

ONCE I WAS COOL

CURBSIDE CS SPLENDOR

CURBSIDE SPLENDOR PUBLISHING

Published by Curbside Splendor Publishing, Inc., Chicago, Illinois in 2014.

First Edition
Copyright © 2014 by Megan Stielstra
Library of Congress Control Number: 2014935169

ISBN 978-1-9404300-2-7
Edited by Leonard Vance
Cover photo by Christopher Jobson
Designed by Alban Fischer

Manufactured in the United States of America.

CS

www.curbsidesplendor.com

It's impossible to say a thing exactly the way it was, because what you say can never be exact, you always have to leave something out, there are too many parts, sides, crosscurrents, nuances; too many gestures, which could mean this or that, too many shapes which can never be fully described, too many flavors, in the air or on the tongue, half-colors, too many.

—MARGARET ATWOOD

This is kind of about you
This is kind of about me
We just kind of lost our way
But we were looking to be free

—PJ HARVEY

CONTENTS

STOP READING AND LISTEN

1

JUST AFTER WE ELOPED and just before the housing market crashed, my husband and I bought a condo across the street from the Aragon Ballroom. If you've never had the pleasure, the Aragon is a legendary music club on Chicago's North Side. Take the Red Line to the Lawrence stop in Uptown and it's the first thing you'll see: breathtaking (albeit crumbling) Spanish architecture, enormous light-up marquee, the line to get in wrapping into the alley, and ticket scalpers on every corner. Here's a fun game: find the nearest Chicagoan and ask them to tell you their Aragon story. Most of us[1] have one or two or five, and many of them go something like this: "Passed out at Rage Against the Machine," "Got peed on at Faith No More," "Broke my arm at Megadeth," "Lots of dudes whipping their penises around in circles at Butthole Surfers;"[2] Profoundly dangerous and/or masochistic crowd surfing and/or mosh pit at KMFDM and/or Deadmau5 and/or Insane Clown Posse, and the classic: "Kicked in the face during Slayer. It was awesome."

But there's more, of course.

There's always more.

So the story(ies) go(es): Capone had underground tunnels running between the Aragon and his favorite bar in Uptown: the Green Mill; good for bootlegging, good for hiding out from the cops, good for those massive secret parties that you always see in movies starring Leonardo DiCaprio. Back then, the Aragon was a ballroom dance hall housing one of the best orchestras in the country; Sinatra played there, as did Tommy Dorsey, Glenn Miller, and Lawrence Welk. Tuxedos and semi-formal—expected. The jitterbug—prohibited. In 1958, a fire next door caused extensive damage, and instead of bouncing back to its former Big Band glory, the Aragon became, in quick succession: a roller rink, a boxing arena, and a discotheque. Then, in the '70s, it housed these crazy, day-long, drunken, furious monster rock shows, thus earning its current nickname of "The Brawlroom" (ball/brawl—see what they did there?). And that, my friends, brings us roaring into the present: mid-sized rock tours, local Spanish language shows, and the occasional boxing match.

You can feel the history in this place. It's peeling off the walls with the paint.

2

I don't know why I bought a condo. The American Dream, I guess. Adulthood. I used the phrase "building equity" a lot, although I wasn't entirely sure what it meant.

3

I do know why I bought *that* condo. It was because of Jane's Addiction. In high school, I was a huge Jane's Addiction fan—still am, but adult devotion is nothing compared to teenage obsession. Fifteen-year-old me had walls papered in *Nothing's Shocking* posters. Fifteen-year-old me brought up Perry Farrell while discussing the great American poets in AP English class. Fifteen-year-old me made out with boys who wore eye makeup.

Thirty-eight-year-old me drinks Cabernet and plays "I Would For You" on repeat.

In November 1990, Jane's Addiction played a somewhat infamous show at the Aragon. At the time, I was a sophomore in high school in small town Southeast Michigan—no way in hell would I have been allowed to go to a concert in Chicago—but I had a sort-of boyfriend who was a few years older (shhhhhh, don't tell my dad) (hi, Dad!), and he made the four-hour drive to be there in his Ford Escort fueled by pop cans we meticulously collected and turned in to the grocery store for ten cents per. "It was awesome!" he told me the next day, his eyes still glazed from no sleep and the glory of the rock. "Perry Farrell climbed the walls! He was up there on the ceiling like a vampire! Everybody was throwing beer bottles, and smashing chairs, and full-body slamming into each other; it was so totally insane, like somebody *must* have died! There's no *way* somebody didn't die!"

"What about the music?" I said.

He looked at me like I was crazy and said, "That was the music."

Fifteen-year-old me didn't have much experience with live shows.[3,4] I hadn't felt the high that comes from *being* there, being *part* of it—the collective energy of the shared experience. My sort-of boyfriend explained it via *Star Trek*: "It's like the Borg—we're thinking and moving and feeling as one," which in retrospect is a pretty fucked-up metaphor, what with their mass assimilation and "*resistance is futile*" and nanoprobes injected into your neck, but at the time?—I totally understood what he meant.

"You can't *get* it unless you're *in* it," he said, and that's how I wound up in the audience for the first ever Lollapalooza tour. It was August 4th, 1991, a few days before my sixteenth birthday. That summer, I'd been at an eight-week theater program at sleepaway camp—yeah, I said it, *sleepaway camp*—and for some reason my parents gave me permission to spend the day at the Pink Knob Amphitheater[5] in Clarkston, Michigan. I remember bits and pieces, a fast-changing montage of image and sound: Siouxsie and the Banshees, Nine Inch Nails, Ice-T; Butthole Surfers (no swinging dicks, FYI) and Living Color. Color! Wild clothes. Tattoos and piercings and mohawks, none of which I'd seen before. It rained for a bit; thousands of people danced in the mud. It was the first time I heard Henry Rollins, who performed his set with his back to the crowd, bent at the waist, and singing into a hand-held mic with his head between his knees. When the Violent Femmes played, the entire audience sang along to that part in "Kiss Off" that goes, "and ten, ten, ten, ten for everything, everything, everything!"

Later, after the sun set over the main stage, people lit bonfires across the lawn, and Jane's Addiction took the stage. The sort-of boyfriend had splurged for pavilion tickets;[6] in my memory I can see the band's buttons and sweat and guitar strings. The night was warm and perfect. I remember standing on my seat. I remember screaming my head off. I remember dancing and not caring what I looked like while I danced—a freedom I haven't felt in decades. The song I most wanted to hear, "Summertime Rolls," was the third one they played that night, and when I heard its lilty, steamy opening bassline, I felt—

Maybe you'll think I'm corny as hell, but what I felt was joy.

This was the one I played over and over, alone in my bedroom on a scratched CD. This was the one I listened to when I fell asleep at night. This was *my* song—the one that spoke directly to *me*—and here I was with fifteen thousand people who felt the same way. Fifteen thousand people, all of us singing.

Me and my girlfriend
Don't wear no shoes
Her nose is painted pepper
Sunlight
She loves me
I mean it's serious
As serious can be...

Fifteen thousand people—fifteen *thousand*—all sharing the same moment.

Maybe this essay can share it with you.

Can you hear it?

Stop reading and listen.

4

I moved to Chicago in 1995 after detours in Boston and Florence, Italy, that were admittedly ill-conceived (why did I go to that college? Why did I go to that country? Why do we do any of the crazy things we do?), but ultimately pretty great insofar as learning about the world and myself—coming of age and whatnot. I was dying to go to the Aragon, to stand inside the place where Perry Farrell had climbed the walls, but I'd only just turned twenty— still a year before I could legally get in. Somewhere during that time, my roommate started dating a guy who lived on the same block of Lawrence Avenue, and long story short: while the two of them hung out, I'd lean against the side wall of the Aragon and listen to the shows.

Weezer. Ozzy Osbourne. Reverend Horton Heat. Lenny Kravitz. Alanis Morrisette circa *Jagged Little Pill.*

It was *awesome.*

It was also, as I've been told on multiple occasions, stupid. Uptown had a reputation, then and still, for gang activity. It's also home to support services for many who are mentally ill. Also: lots of bars, which means lots of drunks. So why was a girl like me, young and alone and naive as hell, standing on a street corner in a place like Uptown?[7]

I never thought of it as a street corner. I thought of it as a rock concert.

More often than not, after I turned 21 and started going to shows inside the Aragon, I'd pretend that I smoked so I could go back out. On warm nights—cold ones, too; it's hot in there and there's no A/C—they throw open the windows, and the music bleeds into the air. I'd lean against the east side of the club, facing Winthrop, and feel the speakers vibrate through the ground and into my shoes. No one elbowed me in the jaw. No one dumped $2 PBRs down my shirt. Inevitably, I'd stare at the building across the street, with its crumbling yellow brick, its iron balconies, its turret. *I want a turret someday*, I'd think.

Two decades and 6.25% financing later, I had that very one.

5

Recently, I was doing some work in a coffee shop, and at the next table I overheard a conversation between a young couple and their relator about the condo they'd just viewed. How it was everything they'd dreamed of and more. I wanted to lean over and say, Hi. Excuse me, sorry to interrupt, but you know that dreams change, right? And markets—they change, too. And some-

times the developer fucks up the roof to the tune of hundreds of
thousands of dollars, and when they rig the building's electricity the wires stretch across your neighbors' backyard and they
try to charge you to *rent their air* and lawsuitlawsuitlawsuit and
yeah, sure, fine, at the beginning you can afford the mortgage on
you and your husband's four jobs, but property taxes go up, and
assessements go up, and you have to fix the roof, and you get
pregnant, and the market crashes, and maybe you get sick, maybe
you have a tumor or some shit, so you and your husband work
more—you add more teaching gigs 'cause that's what adjuncts
do and he signs on to a cubical job that slowly, over eight years,
drains him like an I-fucking-V but hey, it's the American fucking
way, right! and you're so, so lucky to have the jobs and so, so
lucky to have the insurance and so, so lucky to have this beautiful, healthy little kid bouncing off the walls and your poor, kind
neighbors downstairs[8] are so patient with the bounncing and the
banging and the jumping, but still, you're saying, "Baby, don't
jump," like nine hundred times a day and is that the parent you
thought you'd be? and one time, the time that lives in your memory as The Last Straw, you open the closet door and squirrels jump
out and go running around your living room and your kid's like,
YAY SQUIRRELS! and you're like OMG RABIES! and people, as you sit
here with your relator talking about dreams and imaginary num-
bers, my question is this: have you really thought this through?
I mean *really?* Not the "We hooked up, moved in together, got a
dog, got married and now we're supposed to buy a place 'cause
that's the American Dream" sort of thing, because what if that
dream *changes?* What if that dream is changing, right now, this
moment, a plot-point on our historical timeline about privilege
and ownership and societal norms and *do you really want to buy*

this condo? I mean, far be it from me in the safety of hindsight to tell you what you should and should not do but man, if I could yell back across time to my younger self, I'd tell her, Honey— *Rent.*[9]

6

But hey—focus on the good, right? Here's what was good about that condo across the street from the Aragon:

1) My son was born there.

2) My neighbors were awesome.

3) Turret!

4) Sitting on that balcony, three stories above street level, listening to shows. On warm nights, they throw open the windows and the music, suddenly free of the four walls containing it, explodes into the streets. Makes me think of Pandora's Box: all that fury and rawness and savagry and hope hitting the air and becoming our breath. God, I loved it out there. Instead of $2 PBRs, I could pour a glass of wine. Instead of taking an elbow to the jaw, I'd eat popsicles with my kid and tell him about the bands.

"Who's playing tonight?" he'd ask.

"Megadeth," I'd say.

"Death is a band?"

"The Flaming Lips," I'd say.

"We don't lick the stove."

"The Pixies," I'd say.

"Pixies have glitter dust in their butts."

On that balcony, we heard Kim Deal play the opening notes of "Debaser" during the Pixies' 2009 *Doolittle* 20th anniversary tour. We heard LCD Soundsystem do "Daft Punk Is Playing At My House." We heard Morrissey, Johnny Cash, M.I.A., and a gazillion others.

7

During the years we lived across from the Aragon, I stopped being a part of the audience. Instead, I watched them. Up there, I had a front row seat.

When Rob Zombie played, his crowd refused to leave. They mobbed the street, blocking traffic both ways down Lawrence Avenue, chanting "*ZOMBIE! ZOMBIE!*" (I wish they'd been talking about actual zombies. That would've been awesome). Some guy who used to play with The Grateful Dead headlined a show, and forgive the generalization, but the whole neighborhood had a contact high. I remember when the show let out at 2 a.m., and we woke up to a wicked ten-guy pile-up in the street. This happened a lot: the fighting and yelling and drunken brawls; the punching and swearing and bloody noses. But this was the first time everyone involved was wearing tie-dye. My husband opened the window and yelled, "Aren't you guys supposed to love each other?" Kid Rock's fans backed away when they saw him, parting like the Red Sea as he walked the block from his limo to the front door. President Obama had his 50th birthday party at the Aragon, and the Secret Service wouldn't let us leave our building. When they filmed the club scene in *Public Enemies*, they wrapped a chain-link fence around the block to protect Johnny Depp from screaming women. When the Yeah Yeah Yeahs played, I couldn't get off the L. When Weezer played, I couldn't get off Lakeshore Drive. The week I came home from the hospital with my new baby, born three weeks early in the middle of a snowstorm, Marilyn Manson played.

His audience broke a tree in front of my building.

They broke a *tree*.[10]

8

I'm interested in audience. How we come together, feel the high of *being* there. For years, I wrote mainly for live performance; specifically, live performance in bars. The audience is *right there*. So is the laughter, the gasps, and blank faces if I've lost them. When I sit down to write, that's what I'm imagining: the connection, the energy, and the collective electricity of joy or shock or empathy.

The essay was first named by Michel de Montaigne as "Essais," which means "attempts." I like that—an attempt. Here's my attempt to try out an idea. Here's my attempt to figure out what I think. Here's my attempt to show you what I've seen, to share that experience with you. Sometimes, those experiences are fun; the wild and the edgy, the young and the stupid and the free.

But there's more to the story.

There's always more.

9

Yelling and fighting at 2 a.m., immediately followed by gunshots. My husband called 9-1-1, and we watched out the window 'til the sirens came; first police, then fire trucks, then an ambulance. Our bedroom was filled with red and blue light. A small crowd collected on the sidewalk next to the Aragon, and later, we'd find out a teenage boy had died. I wish I could say it was the first time it had happened. I wish I could say it was the last.

An hour later—quiet now, and dark—I got back into bed and began the tricky, foggy work of talking myself back into sleep. I don't know how long I was out before the crying started. No, not crying—that word's too weak; this was a wail. A male voice, wailing. Low and desperate and destroyed, deep at the base of his throat. Maybe at first, I dreamt it, but soon I was sitting up, fully awake, and back to the window.

Three stories below, the boy's father stood where his son had been shot. He stood there all morning—3 a.m., 4 a.m., 5 a.m.—and the whole time, he wailed. A single, raw sob; a few of beats of silence; then another. It made me think of contractions—the pause between the pain. My husband and I sat on the bed, wide awake and listening. We sat there in all of our privilege: our newborn son alive and healthy and asleep in his tiny turret bedroom; our safe, warm home; our middle class upbringings and middle class lives, our education and jobs and insurance; our families; our skin color; our faith; all of it so enormous and so puny in the face of all that pain. I considered reaching into the nightstand to grab the little foam earplugs I used sometimes when the Aragon opens its windows because sometimes the noise is too much, the music and the traffic and the violence and the loss. It's easier to drown it out, to change the channel, to read something else, to believe the same old story, to stick my fingers in my ears and say *Lalalalala* instead of listening to a grief I couldn't fathom and the truths in the world that I don't want to see.

I sat there, listening.

I imagined people awake, listening, up and down the block. Awake, listening, all across Uptown. Awake, listening, across the city, maybe the country.

Are you awake? Can you hear it?

Stop reading and listen.

10

Just after we had a baby and just before we could no longer afford our mortgage, I passed a woman and her daughter standing in front of the Aragon. The mom was in her mid-forties, in Capri pants and a sweatshirt that said GAP. She clutched her purse in both hands and stared up at the Aragon. Her eyes were wide. Her mouth was dropped open. I think she may have gasped. I remembered the first time I saw the Duomo in Florence, or the Fred and Ginger house in Prague, how tiny I felt in the face of all that beauty, all that history—and I looked up at the Aragon, too. I'd been living across from it for nearly three years. It had become part of my every day, and I couldn't remember the last time I really saw it.

What a mind-blowingly beautiful building. Mosaic tilework lines the walls, with concrete vines running up to sculpted faces that sometimes smile and sometimes frown. In its day, this place was the most famous dancehall in the country, packing in eighteen thousand people a week. Eighteen *thousand.* It survived prohibition. It survived the Great Depression. Lawrence *Welk* played there. So did B.B. King. So did The Doors, The Kinks. And Jane's Addiction in 1990, when I wasn't much older than the girl standing next to me on the sidewalk.

She was fourteen, maybe fifteen, and in that painful, awkward vortex of *OMG gross I'm with my mom.* Too much foundation over acne scars. Too much Abercrombie & Fitch. Too-huge headphones jutting out like Princess Leia buns. She held an iPhone in front her face—texting, maybe? YouTube?—and was completely oblivious to her mother, the Aragon, me watching the both of them, and all of Uptown surrounding us: people rushing to work, traffic rushing by, colored chalk pictures on the sidewalk, pigeons pooping on every damn thing, the L train thundering above, radios with the bass turned all the way up, dogs and kids and runners and commuters. And three stories above us, in the yellow brick building across the street, my newborn son was fast asleep in his turret.

The mom nudged her.

She glanced up.

The mom spun her fingers by her ears—the universal gesture for *take off the goddamn headphones.*

The daughter rolled her eyes, but she did it.

The mom put one arm around her (*puke, OMG gross*) and held out the other like she was going to hug the building. "This," she announced, "is the Aragon Ballroom." Her voice held a profound sort of awe, as if the Aragon was the Vatican.

The daughter rolled her eyes again. I'm not sure if the mom noticed; if so, she ignored her, and went on to say the coolest thing in the entire universe.

"I saw a band play here called Jane's Addiction."

Part of my brain may have exploded.

She was in her forties, in a GAP logo sweatshirt with helmet hair. In my head, I'd slapped her with every possible generalization: *suburbs, tourist, old, out-of-touch, uncool,* everything I promised myself I would never become. Not once had I considered that there might be more to her story. That there is always more to our stories. She'd *been* there! She'd been *there,* ducking beer bottles and crowd-surfing while Perry climbed the walls. I wanted her to describe it, to put me there. I wanted to feel the music vibrate through my shoes.

But before I had a chance to ask, her daughter said, "Jane's Addiction? Who's that?"

I left before I flogged her.

11

Upstairs in my condo, I went into the turret to look in on my napping son. Inside, it's not a perfect circle. More like a quarter-piece of pie; two flat walls meet at a right-angle connected by a ninety-degree curve. Our friend Kat, an artist, set up her ladders and painted a huge red tree, its leaves and branches twisting to the ceiling and reaching around the circumfrence of the room, a forest in the middle of the city. I fed my kid in that forest. I wrote there while he slept. I cried there while he cried, in the months following his birth when I lost myself in the fog, and it was there that I found myself, too; listening to him breath and talk and sing and laugh, the best fucking music in the world.

I put my hand on his sleeping back, feeling it rise and fall. Someday, he might look at me the way that woman's daughter looked at her, and that's okay. He might go to rock shoes at the Aragon, ducking beer bottles and climbing the walls, and that's okay, too. He might read these essays, seeing how I tried and failed and tried again, and, hopefully, how there's always more to the story: mine and his and yours and yours and yours.

And on my grave—he'll know Jane's Addiction.

On my fucking grave.

12

Later that night, I went out onto the balcony and looked across the street at the Aragon's enormous marquee, A-R-A-G-O-N running vertically top-to-bottom. Often, one or more of the electric neon letters are burnt out, spelling A-G-O-N or A-A-G-O or R-A-G-O-N. The club was dark that night, so the streets belonged to the city instead of a rock show. I was out there for a while, watching it; my front-row seat to so much messy beauty.

Then I got out my cellphone and called my son's godfather, my oldest friend, Jeff. "You have to promise," I said when he picked up. "Promise you'll tell him that once, I was cool."

Footnotes:

1. I've lived in Chicago for nearly two decades. Chicagoans have told me that that's long enough to call myself a Chicagoan. I think of myself as such, but in the interests of both full disclosure and hometown respect: hold up your right palm; I grew up about a half-inch west of the base of your thumb. Go Blue.

2. Why, Butthole Surfers? *Why?*

3. Unless we count musical theater, which in this case, I am not.

4. At that point in my life, I'd been to exactly two live concerts: 1) Lionel Richie's *Dancing on the Ceiling* tour with my mom—I remember the band suspended upside down on wires during the finale—and 3) an Indigo Girls show in Royal Oak. It was an outdoor amphitheater, and I was standing in a lovely patch of grass near some tiny, lovely trees—exactly where one should be when one is at an Indigo Girls concert. A very beautiful woman in a flowy skirt and a bikini top came up to me, said, "I love you, pretty girl," and hugged me. Then she went up to the tree I was standing next to, said, "I love you, pretty tree," and hugged it.

5. Apparently DTE Energy acquired the naming rights to Pine Knob in 2002, and it's now called the DTE Energy Music Theatre. But fuck that noise. Pine Knob is Pine Knob. Comiskey Park is Comiskey Park. The Sears Tower is the Sears Tower. Now get off my lawn.

6. I don't know what happened to him. I don't remember how we began or how we ended, and it wasn't 'til writing this essay that I fully grasped what that concert meant to me. Thank you, sort-of boyfriend who took me to Lollapalooza. I am profoundly grateful.

7. I've lived and worked and hung out in many different neighborhoods in Chicago. The only time I ever feared for my immediate safety was in Wrigleyville when the bars closed. A guy chased me down the street, yelling that I should stop 'cause he just wanted to talk to me. Don't worry, he wasn't going to rape me or anything. Why wasn't I stopping? *Why wasn't I fucking stopping?*

8. Dear Katie and Steve: ♥

9. I'd also tell her to talk less and listen more. And to read bell hooks like a decade sooner.

10. Marilyn Manson owes me a tree.

TOTALLY NOT ETHICAL

RECENTLY, I DROPPED A BUNCH OF ECSTASY and went to the symphony. A couple of lifetimes ago, I did this all the time: sinking down in my seat and wrapping the sound around me like a blanket, timpani dancing in my fingertips, the cello section syncing with my heartbeat. But then, what always happens happened: I got a job, got married, had a kid, and woke up one morning suddenly, surprisingly, a grown-up.

What did you do when you realized you were...old?

I bought a ticket to *The Magic Flute*, booked a babysitter, and went to my sock drawer, where I'd hid the three little pills of e a friend had given me years before.

"In case of emergency," she'd said, as if I were going to Africa, and this ecstasy could fend off Malaria. I swallowed them all in the cab on the way to Symphony Center.

Have you been to Symphony Center? On Michigan Avenue, down by the Bean? It's beautiful: rotunda lobby with chandeliers, tons of people dressed in expensive things, women in shiny makeup—as I stared at them, I got hyper aware of the layers of mascara on my eyelashes, like I could see these feather-like things flying in the air when I shut my eyes. It's crazy. You have to try it. Like, seriously. Shut your eyes. Now open them, slowly. Look at the light, do you see swirls? Like a Fourth of July sparkler?

That was me in the Symphony lobby: squinting at the chandeliers, trying to see my own eyelashes. And all of a sudden, I heard it: "Megan? Is that you?"

You've seen this moment in a thousand romantic comedies. The main character has food on her face, or has recently vomited, or is peaking on ecstasy, having not done that particular drug for over a decade, and it's then—at the most inopportune moment—that the last person she'd ever expect to see appears: an ex-boyfriend. An ex-boyfriend's new girlfriend. An ex-boyfriend who never really was a boyfriend, just some old guy I slept with a lot; and I probably shouldn't say old because how old he was then is how old I am now, and I'm not old, right?

Right?

I opened my mouth to say his name, and then realized I didn't remember it. Not his first name, anyway, which is funny 'cause usually it's their last names you forget. What I did remember was this: he'd been my professor.

My ethics professor.

My ethics professor, with whom I'd had an affair.

Totally not ethical, but at the moment, I was *in the moment*; eighteen, and free, desperate to be an adult. My ethics professor was thirty-*five*, which at the time was so totally old! I mean, not old like Dating Your Grandpa old; old like he'd lived. He was *experienced*. An *intellectual*. Technically, he wasn't really my professor; he was my T.A., but back then, I didn't know the difference. It was one of those lecture courses where three hundred eighteen-year-olds cram into auditorium seating to listen to someone waaaaaay at the front of the room talk at them for an hour and a half, and then meet later with T.A.'s to actually learn something. This was the guy who listened to us, who knew our names, who graded our papers, and got us all worked up about empirical truths. His thesis was on Kant's *Critique of Pure Reason*, and he talked about it with so much passion—pacing the room, pounding desks, scribbling on the blackboard. Also, he wore really tight pants, so whenever he'd turn his back, all the girls in our group would lean into the aisle for a better view.

Later, in his apartment, after a couple joints, he'd talk just as passionately, except instead of jeans and blazers, he'd be naked, and instead of Kant's *Pure Reason*, it was Zeppelin's *In Through the Out Door*. This was a man who loved Led Zeppelin. He had very involved theories about the philosophical placement of their lyrics, none of which I can remember because I was stoned for the entire duration of our relationship—if you could call it that—and I'm not the kind of stoned that can process complex thought; I'm the kind of stoned that stares at the orange juice cartons like *OMG! Have you ever really looked at one of these? They're amazing!*

Then I giggle for a half hour and fall asleep.

After a few months of this, he asked what I was going to do with my life. We were lying on the couch, on top of a sheet. We were always on top of sheets. He'd gotten divorced the year before and had to get new stuff, so he ordered entire rooms straight out of the Pottery Barn catalogue and then refused to take the price tags off.

It never occurred to me to ask why.

It never occurred to me to ask a lot of things. For example: Did he read the papers he gave me A's on? Was I the only student he invited home? Who exactly was the baby in the photos taped to his fridge, that chubby little girl with his same eyes?

What was I going to do with *my* life?

What had he done with his?

But I didn't say that. I giggled, as though the question were an orange juice carton.

"I'm serious," he said, dragging the joint. "What will you study? How will you live, eat, pay rent?" He didn't *quite* sound like a dad, but he certainly didn't sound like a boyfriend. He sounded like a professor giving a test, as though my dreams were something I needed to list like chapter headings from Immanuel Kant. And suddenly, when I looked at him, I didn't see that experienced adult.

I saw a guy with a receding hairline.

"What I'd like to do—"

I could've said a thousand things in that moment, and all of them would've been true. I'd like to travel—Florence and Thailand and Prague. I'd like to write books. I'd like to fall in love a thousand times. Live hard and desperate and full, my pulse pounding like a bass drum. And when I wake up one morning suddenly, surprisingly, a grown-up, I'd like to be sure in the knowledge that I enjoyed it. Every fucking second.

"What I'd like to do—" I said again, and he leaned forward, excited. It was the first and last time he ever really listened to me. "I'd like to sing with Led Zeppelin."

Then I giggled for a half hour and fell asleep.

Now, a couple of lifetimes later, we were standing in the rotunda of the Chicago Symphony Center. The chandeliers were singing—a thousand cicadas around us; I could feel them in my veins, and my professor was saying, "John," and pointing to himself.

"John!" I repeated. "John!" I was stammering. You don't want to stammer when you run into an ex. You want Be Articulate. And Look Hot. "What are you doing in Chicago?" I asked, relieved to have come up with an appropriate question. And that's when he introduced me to his daughter, a freshman at Northwestern with his same eyes. I thought of saying, *Oh! I saw your baby pictures on the fridge after your dad and I made out on his couch!*—but instead, I marveled at her. She was eighteen, free, desperate to be an adult, and I wanted to yell across time to myself at that age: *Enjoy it. Every fucking second.*

"So—" John said, and I physically lifted my focus from his daughter's face to his; in his Fifties now, his skin a matrix of dips and slopes. "Did you ever sing with Zeppelin?" he asked, and we laughed, because—really—it was hilarious: him and me running into each other after all these years. I was standing at the symphony looking my past right in the eye.

I thought of all I'd done between then and now: traveling to Florence and Thailand and Prague, living and studying enough to later write and teach, falling in love so hard that sometimes I can barely breathe, seeing my husband's eyes in our son's. And when I woke up one morning suddenly, surprisingly, a grown-up.

What did you do when you realized you were lucky?

The light turned on and off, signaling the beginning of the performance, and I said my goodbyes and found my seat. The crowd applauded as the conductor entered, settling himself in front of the orchestra. Then, silence—I'd never heard so loud a silence—and he lifted his arms. This is the moment when, back in my twenties, I'd sink and drown and hide, burying myself under all that sound. But now? Now I leaned forward, excited, anticipating the explosion of all those instruments. And then, for some reason, I turned away from the orchestra and, instead, looked at the line of audience next to me—this wide sea of people, all of us flying.

CHANNEL B

FOR THE FIRST FEW MONTHS after my son was born, I just called him "The Baby," or sometimes "Him" with a capital H—huge proper nouns to illustrate how completely he took over my life. Is he eating, not eating? Pooping, not pooping? What color is the poop? How long ago was the poop? Did I mark the poop on the spreadsheet? I had *spreadsheets.* I had stuff—white noise CDs, magnetic blocks, and this super high-tech video monitor with a remote wireless screen and night vision, which made The Baby glow electric green in the dark like he was a C.I.A. target. It was a little unnerving, actually. It had two frequencies: an A channel and a B channel, in case you had two kids in separate rooms, and what's interesting about this is that one of my neighbors must have owned this same monitor, because on Channel A, I saw my baby, and on channel B, I saw someone else's.

And if I could see someone else's, then someone else could see mine.

At the time, we lived in a third-floor walk-up in Uptown surrounded by other third-floor walk-ups. Jumping onto a neighbor's Wi-Fi signal wasn't much of a stretch, so perhaps the fact that I could toggle between babies shouldn't have been so surprising. But it was. It was huge. I was obsessed. On one hand, it was totally creepy—stalking even—but later, after I got used to the idea... It became sort of magical, like walkie-talkies and CB radios when you're a kid—connecting with someone across the void, adding your voice to the collective unconscious, feeling less alone in this crazy world, and who knows who might be listening?

Who knows who's in that Uptown condo on Channel B?

A baby, to be a sure. But it wasn't the baby I was obsessed with. It was the mother.

My imagination went wild when I thought of the mother. Did she sit there, watching my kid in the dark? Did she question his bedtime? Wonder where I got his pajamas? How might she react if I left a sign in his crib that read: STOP LOOKING AT MY BABY, YOU FUCKING VOYEUR!

Or this one: YAY NEW FRIENDS! DO YOU WANT TO MEET UP AT THE PARK?

Or this one: I AM TERRIFIED. I AM SO TERRIFIED THAT SOMETIMES I CAN'T EVEN BREATHE.

Any winter in Chicago is a force to be reckoned with, but 2008, if you recall, was like The Ice Planet of Hoth. Remember Hoth from *Empire Strikes Back*? Luke almost freezes to death, but Han Solo pushes him inside a dead tauntaun for body warmth? THAT Hoth, and The Baby was born right in the middle of it. My husband, Christopher, had to dig out our buried car, shovel the alley, and navigate Lakeshore Drive though a white-out blizzard. And that relentless, pounding snow stayed through January, February, March, and into April. I am part-time college teacher—no paid maternity leave—and since I'd taken the winter term off to be with The Baby, Christopher, a web designer, picked up extra projects to cover the difference. He worked all day, came home, and went back to work—sleeping three, maybe four hours a night—all while carrying the mortgage, the bills, The Baby—and me.

"Christopher," I'd whisper, middle of the night, night after night. "The baby's not breathing."

We'd be in bed, Christopher lit from the blue glow of his laptop, building some website; me staring at my electric green, swaddled-up pretzel of a Baby. Ever since we'd moved him from our room to his own, that 5x5 inch screen was the center of my universe. Was The Baby sleeping? Was he moving? Was he breathing? He's not breathing!

"Honey," Christopher would say. He was so tired. He was trying so hard to be patient. "The Baby is fine."

"The Baby is not fine."

"He is."

"He can't breathe!"

"Megan—you need to sleep," he'd say, which was true, of course, but have you read the Internet lately? Do you know what can happen to an infant if its mother turns her head for even a fraction of a second? Somebody's always getting crushed under a Bungo or a Bipbap, or being abducted from their own backyard—thank you every episode ever of *Law & Order SVU*—and did you know some kid in the UK just got dragged off by a jackal?

I joke about it now, but the truth is this:

I was scared to sleep—The Baby might suffocate.

I was scared to go outside—The Baby might freeze.

I was scared he wasn't eating, wasn't latching, wasn't gaining, wasn't doing what the books had said he would do, and one day, after a particularly awful bout of screaming—him—and crying—both of us—I looked in the mirror and wondered who that girl was looking back. I was unbrushed, unwashed, and wearing the same yoga pants and empire-waist shirt every day. We all have things about ourselves that we know to be true, and suddenly I couldn't remember any of them. I couldn't write. I couldn't laugh. I couldn't connect with my friends.

I couldn't *see* myself.

At the time, my understanding of postpartum depression was primarily shaped by Brooke Shield's memoir, *Down Came the Rain*: crippling depression and suicidal thoughts. But since what I was experiencing, while heavy, didn't seem *that* heavy; dark, but not really *that* dark; scary, but not, you know, like *that*—it didn't occur to me to ask for help. I mean, I wasn't going to hurt my kid. I wasn't going to hurt myself.

Right?

Now, four years later, I know that the symptoms and intensity of postpartum depression are as varied as the flowers in a greenhouse. I wish I'd told someone. I didn't need to feel that alone; just me in the frozen Chicago winter with my tiny, fragile baby.

And Channel B.

Whenever The Baby would fall asleep, I'd stare at his Day-Glo body on the monitor, making sure he wasn't suffocating—or levitating, or being dragged away by jackals, or whatever hor-

rible thing I'd imagine—and then, once assured of his safety, I'd
flip the channel to see how that Other Mother was doing. Maybe
her kid was eating. Maybe she changed clothes occasionally.
Maybe, for her, snow wasn't a terrifying apocalypse but rather
a Hallmark-like sprinkling of picturesque flakes—"Walking in a
Winter Wonderland," if you will. And yes, I know, it was completely intrusive and unethical and above all, ridiculous. Why
was I comparing myself to this woman? I never even saw her!
Mostly, there was just an empty crib. Sometimes there was a
baby, wiggling and doing baby things, but the mother was a
total non-entity. Until one night, I flipped over to Channel B
and heard crying. Not from the baby—he was fast asleep, an an-
gel—but somewhere in his room, a woman was sobbing. Heavy,
gaspy, gulpy sobs.

They went on.

They went on and on.

I shouldn't have listened.

But it was the first time since my son was born that I didn't
feel alone.

What finally changed things was spring. Birds! Green things!
Grilling on the porch! Frozen blender drinks! Short skirts! Outdoor seating! Lemonade! Which you can get any time of year,
but it tastes better in the sunshine! Sunshine! My God, how desperately I'd needed it! I'd wager most Chicagoans feel this way
in spring, but for me, May 2008 was a Godsend; a great, mammoth hand reaching down out of the clouds and pulling me to
my feet.

That May, The Baby became Caleb—smiling, laughing, re-
sponding; four months old and learning about the world outside

my lap. I'd strap him in a backpack and walk through Uptown: Broadway to Argyle, down to the beach and back up Montrose, finding magic in everyday things. Plastic grocery bags: amazing. Tapping a glass with a spoon: kick-ass! Water in a dish: fun for hours! One morning he reached for a yellow street cleaning sign stapled to a tree, and suddenly I saw yellow as if I'd been blind to it for years:

Brake lights!

Parking lanes!

Taxis!

Flowers in a yard!

Lady in a yellow shirt pushing a stroller!

I stopped. She was pretty—early thirties, wearing yoga pants, and the yellow shirt had an empire-waist. She looked tired. And interesting, like there were all sorts of secret things about her that were set on pause for the time being.

She looked like how I saw myself.

We nodded at each other in solidarity. This, I had newly discovered, is the way moms do it: acknowledging the fact that even though you don't know each other, you're still a part of this great cosmic team—and then you check out each other's kid. Hers was grabbing his toes in the stroller—so sweet. So adorable. So...*familiar.* I looked closer: yes, I knew this kid, and suddenly I saw him not all face-to-face on Lawrence Avenue, but electric green on a tiny hand-held screen.

I looked back at the mother.

"You know—" I started, then stopped, because, really, what would I have said?

STOP LOOKING AT MY BABY?

YOU WANT TO MEET UP AT THE PARK?

How about the truth: YOU HELPED SAVE ME.

"Your baby is beautiful," she said.

"So's yours," I said.

We stood there.

We stood there long past what is appropriate for strangers. I like to think it's because she was thinking the same thing I was. That maybe she, too, had flipped channels in the middle of the night, trying to connect with someone across the void or feel less alone in this crazy world. Maybe she'd overheard me crying in Caleb's bedroom, months ago when everything still seemed so cold.

"How are you?" I asked her. I wasn't just saying it; I really, really wanted to know.

She smiled. "I'm getting better."

"Me too," I said. "I'm getting better."

It was something about myself that I knew was true.

UNDER YOUR FEET THEY GO ON GROWING

IN HIGH SCHOOL, a guy in my English class told me he was having recurring dreams about waking up as a giant cockroach. I thought that was really fascinating, so I made out with him in the prop room after play practice. A couple months later, we read "The Metamorphosis," and I realized he'd used Kafka to get in my pants. This was, of course, not the first time in history that literature has been used for such purposes, and it certainly won't be the last. But it is my first memory of Kafka, his starting point on the line of my life.

My first year of college, we read "The Metamorphosis," *The Trial*, and several critical essays. I remember thinking that the sentences were too long. There was too much description. And what's the bug supposed to mean, anyhow? Is the bug God? I thought the whale from that other book was God. How come everything is God?

I transferred to an American school in Florence, Italy, because why not? I worked as a figure model for drawing classes and read Dante (really long sentences. Lots of description. Does God really mean God?). One day, in an English bookstore, I found a used copy of Kafka's *The Complete Stories*. I can't tell you how many times I read it, but sometime during that book, I decided I didn't want to study literature anymore. I wanted to write it.

I transferred to an art school in Chicago that had a Fiction Writing Department—a place committed to treating writing as an art form, same as dance and painting and theater. For one of my first papers—on Kafka's "The Bucket Rider"—I wrote about historical context, global poverty, and why I thought the story sucked. My teacher handed the paper back, asking me to instead consider place, point-of-view, movement, and how these aspects of craft informed my own work.

It was the first time I'd thought about how a story was crafted.

I left every class wanting to run home and write.

Sometimes, you have to read a story ten, twenty times before you really get it. I was on the L, on my way to a bartending job I hated, reading "The Metamorphosis" yet again, and I had an epiphany—light bulbs appearing overhead, choir of angels coming forth from the Heavens; the whole nine yards—*Gregor doesn't want to go to work, either! So he turns into a bug!* I spent the whole day imagining everything I could turn into instead of working at that bar: a dragon, a British spy, a tidal wave of molten lava.

I've since read "The Metamorphosis" about a thousand times, and I always get it in a different way.

Not long after, I wrote my very first story that I ever considered good. It happened all in one sitting, late at night and into the early morning, in a very similar way to how Kafka wrote "The Judgment":

"The fearful strain and joy, how the story developed before me, as if I were advancing over water" (*Diaries* 212).

My story was about a woman who woke up in bed with The Incredible Hulk. I figured, hell, if Kafka could wake up as a bug...

It was eerie: I'm sitting in a coffee shop, reading "In the Penal Colony," thinking, *Kafka, What the hell even is this? The 'Harrow'? What the eff is a 'Harrow'?* And as soon as the words ran through my head, I got to the next sentence in the story: "'The Harrow?' asked the explorer. He had not been listening very attentively" (*The Complete Stories* 142).

I looked up to see if Kafka was watching me.

He wrote that story in 1914, and here he was in my head nearly a century later.

I kept reading, and every time I was confused or lost or questioned the action, the explorer character would jump off the page and ask exactly what I was thinking.

"'And how does the sentence run?' asked the explorer" (142).

"'But he must have had some chance of defending himself,' said the explorer" (145).

"'I do not approve of your procedure,' said the explorer" (159).

At the time, I had no idea how Kafka pulled that shit off, but since I've started paying attention, I see the technique used everywhere: books, TV shows, pretty much every cop movie ever made. The older, jaded detective (usually played by Morgan

Freeman) is showing the hot-headed, dead-sexy rookie (who in my day was played by Brad Pitt, but maybe it's someone else now. I am old) around the precinct, explaining who's who and what cases are still unsolved, and the dead-sexy rookie asks all sorts of questions that are meant for us, the audience.

I've ripped this off many times in my own work, plus a hundred other things I've seen Kafka pull off on the page. It's mind-blowing, what his work has taught me.

What's that line?

When the student is ready, the master appears.

Tell me if this sounds familiar: I was in my mid-twenties. I was lonely. The writing wasn't going well. I probably drank too much and went home with people I shouldn't have gone home with. Then, one day, I'm minding my own business, reading Kafka's "Wedding Preparations in the Country," and I get to this line: "And so long as you say 'one' instead of 'I,' there's nothing in it and one can easily tell the story; but as soon as you admit that it is you yourself, you feel as though transfixed and are horrified" (*The Complete Stories* 76).

Let's try it out, shall we?

Last night, I went to the bar and did something dumb.

You know when you go to the bar and you end up doing something dumb?

Occasionally, when one goes out to the bar, one might do something less than intelligent.

I realized then how often I'd been speaking about myself in the third person, how much I tried to distance myself from my own actions.

Fuckin' Kafka.

For anyone reading this who is, right now, at this very moment, obsessing over someone in a less than healthy sort of way, I invite you to sit down with Kafka's *Letters To Felice* and immediately feel better about yourself.

When I started teaching, I assigned Kafka—*The Complete Stories*, *The Trial*, and the *Diaries*. "I'm already taking a Kafka class," a student said, and I asked to see her reading list. Out of twelve required texts, not one was anything Kafka himself had written; they were all criticism of what he'd written. Twelve—*twelve*—books of criticism.

"This wall is number one," I tell my students, "and the opposite wall is number ten. Imagine two, three, four, five, etc., written on the floor between them. So let's say number one is 'My work is political,' and number ten is 'My work doesn't have anything to do with politics.' Move to wherever you stand." This first time I played this game, I was backed against the Not Political wall.

"I write love stories," I said.

A gay friend of mine was backed up against the opposite wall, and he said, "I write love stories, too."

I thought about that for a beat or two.

Then I walked across the room and stood next to him.

That day I started to consider the impact of my work; not the intention—the *impact*. I'd like to have an impact. I'd like to contribute to a greater dialogue. I'd like my work to mean something, and truly, how the hell do you pull that off? One of the stories I return to as I consider these questions is Kafka's "A Hunger Artist." I stand outside that cage, day in, day out, admiring his fasting, and I see things in myself of which I'm not proud.

In 2003, the stars aligned in some crazy way, and I got a job in a summer Study Abroad program in Prague teaching courses on Kafka. Over the next several months, in preparation, I read everything by and about him—his journals and letters and biographies—and what blew my mind was this: he's an actual person. A genius, yes, but also normal, albeit somewhat freaky, with all sorts of insecurities and problems. It always amazes me to discover that these writers I idolize are really just people. Like if Jesus walked into my living room and asked for a beer. That's what reading Kafka's journals was like.

Kafka is everywhere in Prague. His face is on T-shirts, coffee mugs—anything that can squeeze a few Euros out of tourists. But if you look past all that, you can see he's also in the bricks, the statues, and the chilled mist like a blanket on the Vltava River. You can page through his journals and find the flats he lived in and the bars where he'd read his work aloud to his friends. I sat in the back room of Café Montmartre, imagining his voice. It wasn't hard. They have really good wine at Café Montmartre.

I didn't have much of a religious upbringing, so when I took my students to visit Kafka's grave, we spent a good three hours wandering around this beautiful old cemetery with its mausoleums and overgrown vines and crumbling sculptures, totally unable to find the guy. Finally, we figured out that we were in the Christian cemetery, which is next door to the Jewish cemetery where Kafka is buried.

Looking for Kafka in a Christian cemetery; it was very Kafkaesque.

When we finally got to his grave, my students wrote notes and left them under rocks. A few of them were crying. The air was heavy; history crawled on our skin.

When I got back to the States, I went to the restaurant where I'd waited tables back in grad school and asked for one shift a week for a year. The cash I saved bought me a year to write in Prague. The following summer, when I got off the plane in to teach my Kafka class, I walked straight to the ticket gate and extended my return ticket from six weeks later to a year later.

It was one of the greatest moments in my life.

My boyfriend and I rented a one-bedroom walk-up in Namesti Miru, an idyllic little expatriate neighborhood a two-stop tram ride from Old Town Square. Every day, I wrote in that back room at Montmartre. It was a dream. I'd never written like that before, nor have I since; not in volume or content, inspiration or ease.

We often went to beer tastings, and one night, while my boyfriend got drunk with a tableful of Czech guys, I had the following conversation with an older man who'd been a public school teacher:

HIM: What are you doing in Prague?

ME: I'm teaching Kafka.

HIM: Czech people hate Kafka.

ME: Why?

HIM: He is too depressing. Czech people, we are not depressing! We are fun! Look at how much fun!

We spent a week in Czesky Raj, which translates to "Czech Paradise"—five hundred miles of protected hiking forest with stairs cut into rocks, rolling hills, and beautiful scenery. We were out there so long it got dark, nearly pitch, and we couldn't find our way back. And did I mention we were on ecstasy? Eventually, our feet found the stone staircase back to our hotel, and I thought of Kafka's line from "The Advocates:" "As long as you don't stop climbing, the stairs won't end, under your climbing feet they will go on growing upwards" (*The Complete Stories* 451).

Dude, I thought, *climbing those stairs. Kafka is like... here.*

Sometimes, students tell me they don't like Kafka. His sentences are too long, they say. There's too much description, and what the fuck's up with the bug? That's fine, I say. Who knows what writers will influences our lives and how their work will grow and change for us as we grow and change with it. I've been reading Kafka for nearly twenty years, and every time, I understand him and myself in a different way.

You don't have to like him, I tell my students. *But keep going, now or next week or next year.* I wonder who I'd be if, at seventeen, I'd stopped at too long sentences, too much description, or that fucking bug.

All said and done, here's who Kafka is to me:

When I'm writing—sitting there at my desk, trying to figure out what happens next, getting pissed when the screensaver pops up 'cause I haven't typed anything in so long, getting pissed when rejections show up in my inbox, thinking about giving up, *There's got to be something easier, right?*—Kafka is a Godsend because when you open his *Diaries*, you see this:

"Today, painfully tired, spent the afternoon on the sofa" (*Diaries* 198).

"I will write again, but how many doubts have I meanwhile had about my writing" (237).

"But I will write in spite of everything, absolutely; it is my struggle for self-preservation" (300).

"Read 'In the Penal Colony' aloud; am not entirely dissatisfied, except for its glaring and ineradicable faults" (318).

"My work goes forward at a miserable crawl" (321).

It goes on like that, page after page. He always goes on. He always kept climbing. Up to his dying day, under his climbing feet the stairs grew upwards.

Kafka, Franz. *Diaries*. New York: Schocken Classics, 1988. Print.

Kafka, Franz. *The Complete Stories*. New York: Schocken, 1971. Print.

KICK MS

WHEN I WAS IN THE THIRD GRADE, my elementary school participated in the Multiple Sclerosis Read-a-Thon—an experience that taught me many valuable Life Lessons, starting with how to coerce adults. We'd bully our grandparents for five cents a page, multiply that times *Island of the Blue Dolphins*, and VOILA!

"Isn't that wonderful, boys and girls!" said my teacher, a tiny, nervous lady who'd only ever taught kindergarten. "Reading is wonderful! And curing a horrible disease is wonderful!" On the bulletin board she'd made a construction paper track that said "RACE FOR A CURE" across the top. Each kid got a car to decorate—mine was green with "MEGAN S." in wobbly cursive glitter-glue—and every day we moved our cars ahead depending on how many pages we'd read the day before.

What happened to me wasn't because of the cars; it was the yellow buttons that teachers passed out on Monday. They said, in block letters, "KICK MS!" and everybody was supposed to wear them all week long. Can you imagine? I was a walking target—a soccer ball, a hacky sack. "Kick MS! Kick MS!" everyone yelled, and they did. At first, the kicks were playful, but as the game escalated, it got more vicious. Those kids kicked the *crap* out of me. I'd run to the bathroom crying and wait in a stall 'til the bell rang. Then I'd wash my face so it wouldn't look all red and puffy and go back late to class, sitting gingerly in my seat.

The day I cracked was a Thursday. The teacher was moving cars ahead on the "RACE FOR A CURE" track. "Look at how wonderfully you're doing, boys and girls! Almost everyone is at the finish line!" *Almost* meant me. My car was alone at the bottom of the racetrack while all the others were thumb-tacked in a big pile at the top. Everyone looked at me then—thirty-two pairs of eyes turning towards my desk—and that's when I lost it.

"I'm not reading for Multiple Sclerosis!" I yelled, jumping up and smacking my desktop with two fists. "Multiple Sclerosis can go to Hell!" Then I ran out of class and down the hall to the girls' bathroom, with its counters and toilets and sinks set three feet from the floor for little-kid legs, and cried into brown paper towels 'til my teacher found me.

We had a discussion then. Here's what I remember:

1. "Hell" is a bad word, like "stupid" and "penis."
2. Multiple Sclerosis is bad.
3. Reading is good.
4. Sometimes kids aren't nice. Sometimes grown-ups aren't, either.

When she said that—*sometimes grown-ups aren't, either*—she started to cry, big heavy sobs that fogged up her glasses. Looking back on it now, I wonder what adult-equivalent of kid-cruelty made her lose it in front of a seven-year-old? Was her husband leaving her? Had her mother said the wrong thing? Did the principal just fire her, and this would be her last moment in the girls' bathroom? Whatever it was, all I knew then was I'd never seen an adult cry before. And as I handed her a paper towel, I realized, for the very first time, that life doesn't get easier.

IT SEEMS OUR TIME HAS RUN OUT, DR. JONES

IT WAS THE WEEK BEFORE WE ELOPED. I had a $20 dress from H&M, my best friend was recently ordained at humanspiritualism.org, and there were three cases of Maker's Mark. We were good to go.

"Except for one thing," Christopher said. Christopher, FYI, was my finance—a fact that still sort of blows my mind. Usually guys like him are: a) Taken, b) Gay, c) Dying, or d) A figment of my imagination. Christopher is none of these things. He's wonderful and smart and "together,"—like, he has goals and shit—and he also loves kids and puppies in a very non-sappy kind of edgy, DIY sort of way. And he always, always does the right thing, even in those moments where the right thing makes you want to stick a fork in your eye, which just then, was exactly what he was asking me to do.

"I can't," I said. "I can't tell him."

"You have to," Christopher said. "He deserves to know."

In my head, I listed every possible out and decided on avoidance. "I'll tell him when we get back," I said, but Christopher shook his head. "This is your last week as a single woman. Get your stuff, we're going now."

He drove me to the Music Box: This beautiful, old movie theatre on Southport that only shows classics or arty stuff. It was built in the '20s, I think—really ornate architecture with this huge red velvet curtain over the screen. I found a seat near the front and tried to calm down; there was a grapefruit sized knot in my chest—one part fear and two parts guilt. We'd been together for so long, twenty years almost, and here I was, showing up out of the clear blue sky to say, "I'm sorry, but I just don't need you anymore." I suddenly wondered how he'd react; he is a pretty unpredictable guy, after all. Would he snap his whip around my waist and refuse to let me go? Would he jump on a camel and track Christopher across Chicago? Or would he do something drastic, like look into the Arc of the Covenant until his skin boils off and he eventually explodes?

The lights went down—and there's that feeling right before a movie when you're transported to another life that's the farthest thing from real—the red velvet curtain rose up—my heart was pounding so fast I didn't know if I'd make it through the opening credits—and suddenly, there he was.

We've all had our little crushes on fictional characters. Jake Ryan from Sixteen Candles, right? Maybe James Bond? Annette Funicello? Legolas? I know you all have one, but please understand: Indiana Jones and I were not just some fling; we were the real deal. And please don't say that, "OMG I love Harrison Ford, too!" because, I tell you what, I could give a rat's ass about Harrison Ford. Or Han Solo. Or Bob Falfa. Or John Book, or Deckard, or any of them.

This is about me and Indiana Jones.

We met in my parent's basement in 1986. I was an only child, which means I was pretty lonely but also that I had all sorts of magical powers. For example, on the day I met Indy, there was a thunderstorm, which I'd started with my brain. Anyhow, I couldn't play outside, my folks were upstairs doing whatever horrifyingly boring things parents do, and all there was in the basement was the TV—this tiny, rabbit-eared job that only got one channel. The Saturday afternoon movie: *Indiana Jones and the Temple of Doom*.

The scene that really got me was the one where Indy and the kid from *The Goonies* are in that secret corridor with all the bugs and decapitated skeletons, and the kid keeps setting off booby traps and almost squashes them very gruesomely in the Spikey Room of Death. And I'm all, "Indy, that kid *sucks!* I am so way better than him!" I was up off the couch, talking directly to the television. "I'm not scared of bugs, and also I can teleport and stop moving walls with my mind!" I would've kept listing off my powers, but just then—I know you'll think I'm crazy when I say this, but it happened, I *swear!*—Indiana Jones turned and looked straight at me, like how in the movies the actors talk into the camera. But there wasn't any camera; there was only me, all alone in the basement with my incredible ten-year-old need, and he saw me. He looked right in my eyes and said, "What a vivid imagination."

That was the beginning. We spent most of our time playing in the creek, digging ancient architectural relics out of the mud, and swinging on vines. Eventually, though, I got older. My priorities changed. I didn't want us to play in the mud anymore; I wanted us to...well, I had these feelings, you know... God, how do I word this? "Nocturnal activities," is what Indy always says, and—don't look at me that way! Like you don't have fantasies!

Everybody has them, my psychiatrist says it's perfectly normal, and Indiana Jones is pretty top of the line of I do say so myself.

A. He's a college professor, fluent in numerous indigenous languages.

B. He has a very great hat.

C. Whenever I needed him, he was there.

Valentine's Day, 1995. I was nineteen years old. I wore combat boots, listened exclusively to Nine Inch Nails, and read waaaay too much Sylvia Plath for anybody's health. My boyfriend was Ricky—he had green hair, AND a leather jacket, held together with safety pins. We'd met dissecting frogs in freshman biology, which in retrospect is an appropriate metaphor for our relationship. Anyhow, we had this *discussion* about how Valentine's Day was sap-ass corporate social conditioning designed to subjugate the masses, and we wanted no part. I believe his exact words were, "Cupid can suck my dick."

He was soooo cool.

So. Long story short: we spent the day in a laundromat. Valentine's Day in a Laundromat in Ypsilanti, Michigan—as gray and dead of a town as you could get—and I remember I was pairing his socks when out of the clear blue sky he said, "I'm outta here tomorrow."

I said, "Outta where?" and he said, "Ypsilanti. *There's nothing here for me*"—at which point I put down the socks.

"I'm here," I said.

And he said, "Yeah, about that."

I wish I could say I handled myself well—that I told him off in exceptionally witty dialogue—but it didn't happen. Instead, I threw a tantrum. In the Ypsilanti Wash'n'Go. I said nasty things and threw dirty laundry, trying my damndest to pick a fight, 'cause if he was standing there yelling at me, at least he'd still be standing there. He didn't take the bait though, and after a while just packed up his stuff and left. And I was alone. *In a laundromat in Ypsilanti on Valentine's Day. Washing his clothes so he could me leave tomorrow*—which, in retrospect, is a very good blues song, but at the time it was rock-fucking-bottom. I might've stood there all day, but just then, I heard it: that unmistakable "*Da-da-da-DAAAA! Da-da-DAAA!*" And there he was, Indiana f'ing Jones on a black-and-white TV near the back of the room. I sat on a plastic folding chair, and for the next six hours, I watched the Saturday afternoon Triple Feature.

From then on, whenever I needed a little rescue from reality, he was there.

Like when I dated the alcoholic.

Or the gay guy.

There were many gay guys, actually.

And actors, lots of actors, most of whom had serious substance abuse problems and girlfriends and/or wives—I know! I made stupid decisions, but everybody does, right? That's how we learn to make smart ones—and Christopher, he's the best thing that ever happened to me. We're three years in, and suddenly I'm watching romantic comedies and wearing color and— flowers? I love flowers! Chocolate? *Bring it on!* Think I'm sappy? Fuck yeah, I'm sappy; I want everybody sappy. I want bluebirds on shoulders and walking on sunshine and *reality to be so amazing that you no longer need your fantasy.*

I no longer need my fantasy.

And so, there I was at the Music Box watching *Raiders of the Lost Ark.* It was that scene where Indy and Marion are in the marketplace in Cairo, and the swami guys are trying to kidnap them, so Marion hides in a wicker basket. And while Indy was running around fighting Nazi henchmen, I was slumped back in my seat, rehearsing what I'd say:

It seems our time has run out, Dr. Jones.

You'll always be my greatest adventure.

I'm sorry, Indy, but I just don't need you anymore.

No matter I came up with, I still felt guilty as hell 'cause you know however much it hurts to get dumped, it's nothing compared to hurting someone else. *I can't do this*, I thought. *Not to him*. And I was on my feet, scooting down the row and halfway up the aisle when I heard him.

"Where you going?"

Slowly, I turned to face him—my Indy—staring down at me from the movie screen with his big eyes and stubbly face and beautiful, stupid smile. Behind him, the swami guys had just found Marion's basket and were carrying her screaming all over Cairo, but she didn't exist so far as we were concerned.

"Indiana Jones," I said. "It's been awhile, huh?"

He laughed. "Do you remember the last time we had a quiet drink?"

"Of course! We were waiting to shoot pool at Inner Town Pub, and some asshole tried to cut in line; you caught him with the whip and let him dangle from the ceiling for a while." I felt suddenly nostalgic. "We've shared a lot of good times."

"That's not all we shared," he said, leaning in close so his face filled the screen. "Primitive sexual practices—"

"Indy, stop." I couldn't let this drag on. "There's something I have to tell you, and... it may come as a shock."

"Nothing shocks me," he said. "I'm a scientist."

He waited, still smiling—and even though I hated myself, I knew I had to do it. "I can't see you anymore."

"What do you mean?" he said.

"I'm getting married."

"Holy shit!"

"I know—it's huge! I never even thought I'd fall in love, let alone—" I trailed off when I saw his face; it was hurt but also angry, like in *Last Crusade* when Elsa tries to steal the Holy Grail.

"Boy, you're something!" he said, turning to walk away.

I followed, moving down the aisle closer to the screen. "Indy, come ON," I said. "What do you care?"

He turned back, his face twisted in a scowl. "Now you're getting nasty!"

"You have your artifacts, your adventures—you don't need me!"

"I'm sorry you think so!"

"It's not like we've ever been exclusive! You had Marion and Willie—"

"I can only say I'm sorry so many times."

He sounded so defeated.

"Indy," I said, reaching out to touch his arm, but he jerked it back.

"Please, I don't need a nurse."

I wasn't sure what else to say, so I borrowed from all the guys who'd dumped me over the years: "Fate just isn't on our side."

He laughed in my face. "I don't believe in that magical, superstitious hocus pocus!"

I pointed my finger at the screen and yelled, "Our whole relationship is magical hocus pocus!"

He looked shocked—like that time he was brainwashed into

thinking he was a Fugee High Priest and Shorty burned him with a torch—and I wondered if he'd ever realized how different our worlds were. I looked around the theater at all those faces so in love with Indiana Jones. In an hour and a half, the lights would go up, and they'd return to their lives.

This time, I needed to do the same.

The music started then, low and distant: "*Da-da-da-DAAAA! Da-da-DAAA!*" And I felt a sudden pang of courage. "Indiana," I said, pointing behind me at the doors out to the lobby. "There's a whole world for me out there, and you've got your own in here. Turn around, look!" He did, and saw the giant bearded Samurai dude coming at him, flipping his machete around like he was about to slice Jones in half. "You don't have to fight," I called. "Just shoot him, it'll go much quicker." He did as told and turned back to me. "Now you have to find Marion," I instructed. "Just follow her voice; she's loud as Hell. They're going to try to make you think she blew up in that Nazi truck, but they've really got her stashed away in some tent. Remember that and you'll be fine." He nodded and made as if to rush off, then turned back to face me.

"Sweetheart, after all the fun we've had together," he said, and I smiled.

"We have had fun, haven't we?" I said.

From the surround sound around me, I heard Marion yelling, "*Inddeeeee.*" And then he was off, back to his own world. I pushed open those theater doors and went out into mine: the city, the street, and Christopher parked out front, waiting to drive me off into the sunset.

THE DOMINO EFFECT

ABOUT TEN YEARS AGO, I waited tables at a brunch restaurant in Wicker Park called the Bongo Room, known for its insanely amazing Chocolate Mascarpone French Toast and the insanely large crowds of people waiting to eat it.[1] Every Sunday, these guys would come in—we'll call them Steve, Jim, Mark, and Chip. Steve, Jim, and Mark were cool; they talked about last night at the Hunt Club, dressed head-to-toe in Abercrombie and Fitch, and tried to buddy me up for faster service. "Hi, what's your name?" they'd say when I got to the table. Then, "Hi, Megan! We're Steve, Jim, Mark, and Chip!" I didn't bother saying they'd told me before, told me last week, told me eighteen thousand times, *so can you just get on with the pancakes and Bloody Marys, 'cause the wait for a table is over an hour; the guy at twenty-three is bitching about his benedict; I just got a nine-top on twenty-four, eight of whom want soy lattes—soy, for chrissakes!—and I don't have time to yak it up. So can you order?*

But of course, they couldn't.

"You see her?" Chip said, nodding at a girl a couple tables over. She was *perfect.* Shiny hair, great body, big smile; imagine a television commercial for toothpaste or hairspray.

I looked back at Chip and said, "Yeah?"

"Can you find out if she's married?" he asked, and right away, Steve, Jim, and Mark started laughing. I should point out that Chip wasn't like the other three. He was kinda chubby, kinda balding, kinda boring—like, if I say *tax attorney*, you might imagine a guy like Chip.

"You wanna date *her*?" said Steve, Jim, and Mark. This was always how they treated him—sometimes he was the punchline, sometimes the punching bag. And while usually he'd turn red and laugh along with them, today he gripped the edge of the table and said, "No, I don't want to date her; I want to marry her."

The reaction was immediate:

"That girl wouldn't be caught dead with a guy like you."

"That girl eats guys like you for breakfast."

"An appetizer for the main course, know what I'm saying?"

Chip looked at me.

"Please?" he said.

It was the please that did it.

I went by her table, planning on doing a quick left hand check—ring or no ring?—and then back to Chip with the verdict, but it wasn't that simple. The girl was sitting with her left arm crossed over her stomach and her left hand tucked underneath her right armpit. I watched her for nearly a half hour, and the whole time she ate, drank, and gestured with only her right hand.

"Well?" Chip asked.

"I'm working on it," I said. Then I walked to her table and

dropped a napkin on the floor, squatting down to hands and knees on the ground and looking up at her lap—no go.

"What are you doing?" asked my friend/co-worker, Molly, once I was back in the service station.

I told her.

"That's so romantic!" she said, jumping up and down and clapping. "It's like when you're on the subway, and you see someone, and you lock eyes, and it gets too intense, so you have to look away, and when you look back, *they're* looking away, and what I always wonder is: what would happen if you just kept looking?"

I didn't know.

"We'll *never* know," Molly said, "because nobody ever *tries!*"

Before I could fully wrap my brain around that idea, I saw that Chip's girl was standing up. She was reaching for her jacket. She was dropping her left arm down and, no, there wasn't any ring, *because there weren't any fingers.* There was a hand and some stumps of varying sizes, where fingers ought to be but weren't.

I went to Chip's table. "She doesn't have fingers," I announced.

They looked at me blankly, so I held up my left hand and folded my fingers into my palm. "No fingers," I said again.

Steve, Jim, and Mark nearly died laughing.

"Leave it to you to fall for a—"

"Guess she's not so perfect anymore—"

"The one time you have balls enough to—"

But Chip didn't hear any of it. He just watched as she left restaurant, and then, when the front door closed behind her, he did the last thing you'd ever expect from a punchline or a punching bag:

He got up and ran after her.

About six months later, I was walking around the restaurant refilling coffee and there, at a two-top by the front window, was Chip—who, FYI, looked fantastic; he'd shaved his head, muscled up a bit, and dressed more cutting edge. Like, if I say *CEO of New Social Media Empire*, you might imagine a guy like Chip. It was easy to see the reason behind the change, because sitting across the table from him was—wait for it—the girl. His beautiful, fingerless, perfect girl.

It took everything I had not to cheer.

They told me the whole story: how he caught up with her on the sidewalk; how he didn't know what to say because he'd never done anything like that before, but, dammit, he *tried*; and how, when people ask where they met, they talk about the crazy waitress at the Bongo Room who crawled around on the floor.

Hearing that story, for me, was a gift. At the time, I was single, sort of bitter—just *done with it*. Have you been there? And knowing that these two people were giving it a go—that they were *trying*—had a huge impact on me. Enough to start trying myself. Enough to tell this story over and over to friends of mine in similar situations. Enough to write it for a storytelling series I work with where we tell our stories aloud in the hopes that they will inspire our audience to consider their own, and how—even as we celebrate our differences—there are still multiple connections in our lives.

Here's the power of a story: someone hands it to me like a gift (I imagine it wrapped in shiny paper with the bow, the handmade letterpress card—the whole nine yards). And in that gift, I find parts of myself that have been missing, parts of our world that I never imagined, and aspects of this life that I'm challenged to further examine. Then—and this is the important part; the money shot, if you will—I take that gift and share it. In my own writing, sure, but the kind of sharing I'm talking about here is the domino effect: how I hear/read/watch/ a story and then tell everybody and their mother about it, and then they tell everybody and their mother, and somewhere in that long line of people is someone who, at this exact point in their life, needed its message more than we'll ever know.

We do this all the time: "Oh my gosh, I just saw heard/read/ watched/experienced the most awesome thing! It's called [insert awesome thing][2] and it made me think about—"

What?

What did the last story you heard/read/watched/experienced make you think about?

Did it help you find parts of yourself that have been missing? Parts of our world that you never imagined? Aspects of this life that you're challenged to further examine?

My God—*what a gift.*

And now, you wrap it up and give it away. Somebody out there really needs a good present. Maybe your friend, maybe a co-worker, maybe that random person sitting next to you on a bus.

Or maybe the crazy waitress at that restaurant you go to every single day; the one who's ready to crawl around on the floor if it helps you find the love of your life.

Footnotes:

1. The Bongo Room should also be known for the kindness and generosity of its owners, Derrick Robles and John Latino, whose friendship and business supported me while I put myself through school, made art, kicked off a teaching career, and generally figured out what the hell I was doing. I'd wager there are

many theatre artists, literary artists, visual artists, and artists who can say the same. So, on behalf of us all, I'd like to say thank you to the service industry for helping us pay our rent *and* live our dreams, for allowing us the flexibility to audition and finish projects, for giving our audiences the space to discuss our art over yummy food, for our after parties (!), for coffee, for wine, and—most of all—the lifelong friendships.

2. Anything and everything by Roxane Gay. 2nd Story. The Paper Machete at the Green Mill. Oona... rocks. Kafka. Gabriel Garcia Marquez. *East of Eden. Geek Love. Miles From Nowhere. Why I Fight. Bluebirds Used to Croon in the Choir, Fall on Your Knees, The Temple of Air,* and *Just Kids.* Aleksander Hemon's *The Book of My Lives.* Kiese Layman's *How to Slowly Kill Yourself and Others in America.* Lidia Yuknavitch's *Chronology of Water.* "Three Things You Should Know About Peggy Paula," by Lindsay Hunter, and "Return from the Depot!" by Elizabeth Crane. Anything and everything by Dorothy Allison, but mostly "River of Names," which I saw her read at a beautiful old church/arts center as part of the Sister Spit tour. Hearing Dorothy Allison read, in and of itself, is a sacred thing, but hearing her in a church... It was one of those moments when you almost believe in God. Anything and everything by Cheryl Strayed, but most of all this from *Tiny Beautiful Things*: "You don't have to get a job that makes others feel comfortable about what they perceive as your success. You don't have to explain what you plan to do with your life. You don't have to justify your education by demonstrating its financial rewards. You don't have to maintain an impeccable credit score. Anyone who expects you to do any of those things has no sense of history or economics or science or the arts. You have to pay your own electric bill. You have to be kind. You have to give it all you got. You have to find people who love you truly and love them back with the same truth. But that's all." Anything and everything by Toni Morrison, but most of all this: "I tell my students, 'When you get these jobs that you have been so brilliantly trained for, just remember that your real job is that if you are free, you need to free somebody else. If you have some power, then your job is to empower somebody else.'" Anything and everything by bell hooks. The personal essays published at The Rumpus, Guernica, The Millions, and Electric Literature. Rookie: a website for teenage girls (but also for me). The visual art curated at Colossal. Everything on Brainpicker. Samantha fucking' Irby at BitchesGot-

taEat. Yayoi Kusama's *Obliteration Room*. Anna Schuleit's *Bloom*. Mica Angela Hendricks' illustrations with her four-year-old daughter. *Exposure #42: N.Y.C. Broome & Crosby Streets, 06.09.06, 7:12 p.m.* by Barbara Probst. Those crazy underwater sculptures by Jason deCaires Taylor. Stefanie Posavec. Paul Octavius. Alexy Terenin. Amy Martin. Alison Bechdel. The Sketchbook Project. The You Are Beautiful Project. The part during *The Artist is Present* when Marina opens her eyes and sees Ulay. Zoe Keating. *Don't Let Me Be Misunderstood* by Nina Simone. Anything and everything by Nina Simone. PJ Harvey's "Stories From the City, Stories From the Sea." *Ambulance* by TV on the Radio. Sweet Honey in the Rock. Girl Talk. Mucca Pazza. Scotty Karate. *Summertime Rolls*. That TED talk by Chimamanda Adichie called *The Danger of a Single Story*. The TED talk by Adora Svitak called *What Kids Can Learn From Adults*. The TED talk about dancing your PhD. Jim Coudal's talk at Creative Mornings. Lana Wachowski's acceptance speech for the HRC Visibility Award. Trinity in *The Matrix*. *The Matrix*, period. *The Princess and the Warrior*. *City of Lost Children*. The original *Pitch Black*. The part in LOTR where Legolas slides down the elephant. *The Wire. Firefly. 24. 30 Rock. Homeland* and *House of Cards* and *Veep. The Walking Dead*, both the graphic novels and the TV series #teammichonne. *Game of Thrones*, both the books and the TV series #teamkhaleesi. #teamsydneybristow. #teamoliviapope. Khanisha Foster in *Actor of Color*. Julie Ganey in *Love Thy Neighbor. Liza Minelli's Daughter* by Mary Fons, *Burning Bluebird* by Jay Torrence, and *There is a Happiness That Morning Is* by Mickle Maher starring Diana Slickman #teamslickman. *What's the T?* by the About Face Youth Theatre, and the mighty Young Chicago Authors with *Louder Than a Bomb*. This, from designer Frank Chimero: "Once the work is done, it's not yours anymore. You draw the comic, write the book, make the app, and then it makes its way out into the world. And it starts to talk back to you. It's the weirdest thing—if the thing you make goes anywhere, it's because other people carried it. Your thing becomes our thing. This is deeply unsettling, but it is also a beautiful situation that binds us to one another." This, from the Chicago poet Coya Paz: "The work is enough. I feel grateful I am able to do it, that every day I wake up to a job I love, a privilege afforded the very few and I am wise enough now to know it." And this, from *Letters to a Young Poet*: "a work of art is good if it has sprung from necessity."

WAKE THE GODDAMN WORLD

MAYBE I'M REMEMBERING IT WRONG. It happened over a decade ago, and that's plenty of time for the mind to play tricks. She was screaming—that much is certain—and scared. Right? Wasn't she? It sounded like it, but maybe I'm thinking of all the movies and TV shows and news broadcasts I've seen where the man raises his hand and the woman cowers. Maybe I'm using bits and pieces from those stories to fill in this one.

Here's what I know for sure: It was the middle of the night. I heard screaming. I got out of bed and went to the window. Four stories down, the two of them were in front of our building. There was a street lamp. I saw some, but not all.

There was pushing.

Dull smacking sounds—palm on skin? Fist on bone?

But maybe I'm making that part up.

•

I spent the bulk of 2004 in Prague, teaching Kafka for an American study abroad program. My boyfriend and I paid $500 a month for a one-bedroom walk-up, fully furnished from IKEA, with huge windows that overlooked an idyllic cobblestone street. I hung wet clothes from those windows to dry. Sometimes birds flew in, getting stuck in corners where the ceiling met the walls. One time, I threw coconuts to the ground, four stories below, trying to crack them open. We were making gumbo from a recipe we got off the internet; for some reason, it called for coconuts. Where do you get a coconut in the Czech Republic? "Kokosovy orech?" we asked grocer after grocer, our accents cutting pinpricks into the thick, tongue-heavy Czech. Finally, we found some at the Prazska Trznice and bought them all—an enormous stack of impossible, impenetrable fruit sitting on the counter and taunting us. Our furnished kitchen, with its fully-stocked drawers, held nothing that resembled a meat cleaver. Or a screwdriver. Or a blow torch, or a buzz saw, or a machete.

It was the ultimate defeat.

It's worth mentioning that, at the time, I was starting to feel a bit crazy: a head full of Kafka, homesick, and reeling from the recent U.S. presidential election. It was mid-November, and a permanent gray mist had blanketed the castles and cobblestone, perfect and Goth and mysterious for the first few months, but then—gray. In Chicago, Seasonal Depression is a *thing*; we prep for the winter the way others might for the apocalypse, and for the record, it has little to do with temperature. My brother in Fairbanks, Alaska, plugs his car into a generator every night so the engine won't freeze, and he laughs when I complain about Midwest winters. But truly, the gray is no joke; It slides into your psyche, every month getting darker. By March, we're ready to climb out of our skin. I start to resemble a character from *The Shining.*

I hadn't expected it to happen in Prague, but there I was in the first week of November, throwing coconuts out a four-story window.

•

So, yes, there was screaming. And, yes, pushing. Their bodies were stumbling in and out of the spotlight, so I couldn't tell who started what, who was grabbing who, or who was trying to stay or go. Maybe she wanted to run away and he caught her. That made sense. What father would let his teenage daughter roam the streets in the middle of the night? But maybe, maybe he's a big ol' dickwad, and she was trying to get away from him. There are rules about that stuff in the Czech Republic, right? Were they Czech? They weren't speaking Czech. At least, I didn't think so, but my Czech was pretty shitty, then and always, even after I took tons of classes and did the Rosetta Stone CDs.

How do you say, "My dad's a dick?"

How do you say, "Leave me the hell alone?"

How do you say, "Help me."

Pomozte mi.

Pomozte mi. Prosim.

•

The building we lived in was owned by an older Russian guy who was in his fifties, maybe. He lived on the second floor, rented out the third and fourth floors to expats like us, and ran an audio studio on the first. That's what it was called: *Audio Studio*, stenciled on the front door in English, Czech, and Russian. It consisted of two black pleather couches facing each other in the center of the room, surrounded on all sides by speakers: floor-standing, architectural, and sub/sat systems; source, processing, and amplifier components; two dimension; three dimension. Customers would sit on the couches, and my landlord would blast his favorite songs—think American '80s pop like Bon Jovi and Peter Gabriel and Lionel Ritchie. Now think Bon Jovi and Peter Gabriel and Lionel Richie, all day, every day, over and over, through every possible kind of speaker. I had no idea there were so many—the bass and volume and reverb and vibration, the different qualities of sound.

Renting from him was a bit of a process. He spoke no English; we spoke no Russian. Our transactions were conducted through his daughter—a very lovely, very awkward teenager in ironed blue jeans and pristine white sneakers who was always reading magazines in the corner of the room, always plugged into an iPod, living in her own music, her own world. In the middle of the culture shock, everything so strange and new, this girl felt so gloriously *familiar*; not that long ago, I'd been in those same white shoes—fourteen, fifteen years old—waiting in my parents' living room, waiting for my moment to run free.

When money needed to change hands, either from customers buying speakers or the renters living upstairs, she'd take off her headphones and conduct business in a complicated mix of Czech, Russian, English, and hand gestures, while her father sat on his couches playing "Purple Rain" or "Livin' On a Prayer." Over many months, this girl and I built our own language, yell-

...ng our heads off over the music and passing paperwork back and forth about the rent, the lease, the neighborhood. I remember loving her voice—all that youth and sweetness wrapped around the thick, heavy Slavic. It made me think of boxing—the delicacy of the footwork and the power of the punch.
I wish I could tell you more about her.
There are a lot of things I wish.

•

I didn't know what they were fighting about. I didn't know the language or the cultural norms of Eastern Europe. I didn't know if they were Eastern European. I didn't know where to buy a coconut. I didn't know how to convert money. I didn't know how simple it was to renew a VISA. I didn't know the Czech equivalent of 9-1-1. I didn't know what would happen if I called the police. If he was put in jail, what happened to her? Where would she go? In all the months of living there, I'd never seen a mother. I didn't know if she had a mother. I didn't know if she went to school. I didn't know how old she was. I didn't know a thing about her story, and I didn't know if it was appropriate or acceptable or advisable to ask. I didn't know if she was screaming in fear or fury or both. I didn't know if I was the *us* or the *them*. I didn't know how often I'd think of this moment, trying to fit it all together like a broken vase with superglue, and I didn't know how many pieces were missing—blanks in my memory like a self-imposed force-quit.

•

I love Chicago. The pulse of this place is my heartbeat. I'm raising my child here. Every day, I'm grateful to zip in and out of its grid, and I work to give back as fully and completely as I've been given.

But Prague.

Prague is in my dreams; its streets are the streets I see when I shut my eyes. Every time I trip over something—and I'm stupidly clumsy, so it happens a lot—I can feel Prague in my body, its uneven jags of cobblestone under my feet. Those first several months of living there, so young and free and open, remain the best in my life. In Prague, I was writing. In Prague, I moved slowly, deliciously. In Prague, I was *in love*; the boyfriend and I got together a month before I left Chicago, and we decided he'd come with me, which was a little shocking but also the most exactly right thing. Remember when you first fell in love? You couldn't be apart for more than an hour. You had to have sex *all the time.* You had to make elaborate dinners, drink tons of cheap wine, and stay up all night discovering every ridiculous detail about each other—"You like Philip Glass? I heard one of his songs one time fifteen years ago! Let's make out!"—because everything is so perfectly, so breathtakingly new. One day, he came home from Tesco with a bottle of *Mr. Proper*, which is the same thing as the American *Mr. Clean*, the cleaning liquid. Same product, same packaging, same bald guy on the label. Why is that important? I have *no idea*, except when he told me, when he excitedly showed me the bottle—this vast and profound discovery—I thought he was so fascinating, so intelligent, so totally *the one*. Which he is; so much so that later I married him, but not because of some cleaning product. The cleaning product was part of that initial, magical, lovesick, half-sane haze. And to this day, if you show me a picture or film set in that city, if you quote a line of Hrabal or Macha or *The Book of Laughter and Forgetting*, or if you even mention the word Prague, I'm right back in the haze.

It's been ten years, and still—snap your fingers—I'm right there.

"Are you enjoying your time in Prague?" our landlord's daughter would ask, month after month, taking off her iPod to count our rent.

I didn't know how to answer the question.

I didn't have the language for it.

•

Maybe she wasn't his daughter; that's an assumption on my part. He is older and she is younger, and in the absence of factual information, my memory filled in the blank: Father/daughter. But what about the other possibilities? Employer/Assistant? Let's run with that one. It's nicer, and I'd rather think of nice things than not-so-nice things, things that you read in newspapers or see on *Law & Order SVU*. Like, maybe he bought her on the black market and forced her into prostitution; or maybe he kidnapped her and made her steal speakers and everything in the building is stolen, and the Czech-equivalent of the Feds will raid our apartment any day now; or maybe, maybe they're lovers in a totally gross and unethical fifty-something guy/fifteen-year-old girl sort of a way; or maybe she's not even fifteen—I'm assuming that, too—but if she was, there's no way that shit was consensual—I don't care what Lolita did or not do; *Lolita* is fiction, and this girl was real. She was real. She was screaming on the cobblestone four stories below me, and what should I have done? Called the police? What would I have said? *Hi, nemluvim cesky, no, I don't have a VISA, but something is happening. Can you sem si pospisit prosim, please?*

•

When I first met Marketa, the woman who would become my closest Czech friend, she said, "There is an election soon in your country. Before we may be friends, I must know which you wil vote."

"Kerry," I told her. "I already sent an absentee ballot for Kerry."

"Good," she said. "Now we will do this thing."

It was fall of 2004. The United States government had recently asked the Czech Republic to pledge soldiers to Iraq. Anti-Bush graffiti was everywhere, the international media didn't try to hide their disdain, and it never once occurred to me that he might actually win, which is probably why it hit me so hard when he did. After Kerry conceded the election, Marketa sent me an email that read: "Do not be sad, Megan. I will still be your friend. You are not one of them."

I still have that email; it's a plot-point on the line of my life. It brought to the forefront a tangled conversation about privilege that I'd been having with myself for years, forcing me to set aside everything I'd read, the stories I'd heard, the (what I thought had been) careful and critical listening about culture and nationality and race and difference and *other*, and take a terrifying look in mirror. *You are not one of them.* Aren't I? Who is this all-elusive *them*? The bad them, of course, but is it really that easy? Good and bad, us and them, right and wrong.

Later that day, my then boyfriend/now husband came home from the Internet café to find me throwing coconuts out the window. At first, I'd wrapped them in plastic bags, hoping to save the milk to put in a gumbo, but after the second or third, I didn't care. I wanted to break something. I wanted to get out of my own goddamn head. I wanted to find the right words.

"Are you enjoying your time in Prague?" our landlord's daughter asked, taking off her iPod to count our rent.

I didn't know how to answer the question.

I didn't have the language for it.

•

It was the middle of the night, and I woke up to screaming. I was safe in my bed, safe in my secure job, rent paid, and had a healthy relationship with a kind, gentle man, which is a privilege I hadn't always had, but I had it then and I've had it since. I remember getting out of bed and going to the window, opening it just enough to stick out my head. Four stories below, in front of our building, I saw my Russian landlord—huge and hairy and shirtless in pajama bottoms—and what I first thought was a grown woman in high, high heels. She was still screaming—had been screaming the whole time it took me to wake up, sit up, get out of bed, go to the window, open it, and lean out—and sure, fine, that doesn't take much time. Ten seconds, max.

Imagine what can be done to a body in ten seconds.

Imagine what can be done to a heart.

Imagine what happened before I got to the window, before my eyes adjusted from the dark of the bedroom to the glare of the streetlamp below. They were cast in a nearly perfect spotlight, like a film set or a stage show. She was screaming, first wordlessly, then in Russian, and it was then that I recognized her voice—the delicacy and the power, the sweetness and the punch. I leaned out further and—underneath the more adult clothes, the jewelry, and the make-up—it was unmistakably her. I'd never seen her outside of the building; never seen her without those white,white sneakers; never imagined what her life was like. Did she have a boyfriend? A girlfriend? Maybe she wanted to be a translator, or a teacher, or a rock star. In my memory, she's in school, she's brilliant and funny and works her ass off, and within two years—three, tops—she's out of the Audio Studio and running free, fast as she can away from that awful, awful night. Her heels put them at equal height, and they gripped each other's shoulders. I couldn't tell who was pushing or who was pulling; everything was fast and blurry and loud and louder and I didn't know if she was screaming in fear or fury or both. I didn't know if he was throwing her out or fighting to keep her there. I didn't know who hit who first, but there was no mistaking the fact that he outweighed her three times over. The force of him knocked her off those impossibly high shoes, and there was nothing to catch her but the cobblestone. Her body was bent in impossible directions.

It happened so fast. It was dark. I didn't understand what they were saying. I didn't know the cultural norms of Eastern Europe. I didn't know the Czech equivalent of 9-1-1. If I did call the police, what would I say? *Hi, help, nemluvim cesky. Something is maybe happening, can you sem si pospisit prosim, please?* And what would happen then? If he went to jail, what happened to her? She was just a girl! Wasn't she? She was his daughter! Wasn't she? In all the months of living there, I'd never considered her story, and of course it's not appropriate or acceptable or advisable to ask, right? None of our business, right? Someone's getting hurt below my window; or in the building next door; or on the L; or two neighborhoods over; or in some other city or country or community; and there will always, always, always be a reason to stay silent; always a seemingly good excuse to do nothing. I did nothing.

    I did nothing.

●

The day we moved out, our landlord turned up the bass as high as it could go. I could feel the music vibrate in the walls of our building, up through the floor, and into my shoes. It was December now; we'd been there just under a year. All of our possessions fit into two mountain backpacks, and mine felt unexpectedly light as I went down those four flights of stairs.

    Inside the Audio Studio, Tom Petty's "Free Fallin'" was playing in surround sound. My landlord, per usual, was on the couch with a customer, and the daughter glanced up from her magazine when I came into the room. I don't know what I'd expected. Maybe her arm would be in a sling? Maybe he'd be on crutches? Maybe they'd be wearing sunglasses to hide the bruises? Maybe she'd be long gone?

    "Hi," she said, taking off her headphones and standing up. She was so lovely. So awkward. So fourteen-years-old and almost free to run. "You are leaving Prague now?"

    This is where, in my memory, I apologize, digging through our shared patchwork language to find the right words: *I'm so sorry. I should have done better. I will do better.* I tell her how, this time, I will rush down the four flights of stairs and put my body between theirs. This time, I will rush down the four flights of stairs—not in time to stop it, but still in time to help, to get her to a hospital, or a friend's, or a shelter. This time, I will grab the lamp off my bedside table, a knife out of the kitchen, a bomb out of the bathroom, and I take aim, squinting one eye at the top of his skull, knocking him out from so many stories up. And this time, I will scream. I will be so fucking loud. I'll wake the goddamn world.

THE RIGHT KIND OF WATER

THE FIRST HOUR IS GREAT. I'm in the bathtub, submerged to my neck. The water is warm and lovely, and I'm more relaxed than I've been in months. And the best part? What I'm doing here is work; it's rewriting. It's *research*.

While finishing up final edits on my story collection, I couldn't shake this nagging feeling that one of them, "One One Thousand, Two One Thousand, Three," wasn't right. It was missing something. I read it over a thousand times and couldn't pinpoint what bothered me, which is the fucking worst. If I can name the problem, I can fix it. I can go to my bookshelf, pull down the Garcia Marquez, the Tolstoy, Hubert Selby, James Baldwin, or Dorothy Allison, and figure out the literary gymnastics necessary to make the damn thing work.

Here's the gist: a 13-year-old girl, Eliza, is skinny-dipping in a quarry in Southeast Michigan. She thinks she's alone, but turns out there's a group of high school guys nearby getting drunk in the woods. They discover her. Threaten her. Trap her in that quarry like a cage and demand she get up so they can look at her. Like a lot of fiction—mine, at least—this is based on some semblance of a true experience, and what interested me the most as I wrote it was the tension. Would she stand or wouldn't she? How would they react when she did or didn't? How would she react to their reaction?

I teach creative writing classes, and what finally cracked the issue was a discussion my students and I had around a scene from Don DeGrazia's *American Skin*. Alex, the main character, boards the L, all hell breaks loose, and then he gets off.

"How much times passes between the on and off?" asked one of my students. "Like five minutes? How does the reader see those minutes passing?"

And all of a sudden, I knew. In "One One Thousand...," the story starts when Eliza gets in the water and ends when she gets out. But how much time passes between the two? I didn't know. Later, rereading the story, I saw certain clues I'd placed unconsciously: at the beginning, the sun is high, warming the water; by the end, it's freezing and the stars are out. So that's—what? 3 p.m. to 8 p.m.? Five hours? That's a lot of time for somebody to be naked in the water. What happens to a body when it's submerged for that long?

This is the point where, historically, I hit the library. I'm the stay up all night/drink too much coffee kinda girl, finding esoteric details in random books. Even now, with the Internet, I still stalk libraries, milking electronic reserves for all their worth.

But—

I'd recently published a story set in a greenhouse. I wrote about that greenhouse from memory—blah, blah, plants and trees—adding in fancy sounding names pulled from the 25th anniversary edition of *The Book of Plants*. And then, not long after, I stopped by the Gethsemane Garden Center and realized my description had been totally, completely, utterly wrong. I'd forgotten the tropical temperature; the hoses full of pinpricks, spraying everything with a fine, hot mist; the ceiling of green, like a jungle. I knew then that I needed to up my research game. If I could go there, I'd go. If I could do it, I'd do it. If I could live it, I'd live it.

So.

With no quarries in the immediate vicinity of Chicago, and the late-fall chill already here, I decided on the bathtub. I would sit in the bathtub. For five hours. iPhone alarm set to count down the minutes, journal on the nearby toilet to take notes about my skin, my fingertips, my toes, my teeth (chattering?). I had very vague, very naïve, very uninformed ideas of what would happen, and a silly sense of pride in what I was doing.

Research!

I was so totally a writer!

•

In the second hour, my hands and feet are, predictably, wrinkled. The water is cold and draining slowly, down from neck-level to just below my breasts. More than anything, though, I'm bored. Usually, when I take baths to relax, I either read or precariously prop my laptop on the toilet to watch *Buffy the Vampire Slayer* on Netflix. But this here in the bathtub, this is not relaxation; this is research! Serious research! I'm experiencing what Eliza experienced, feeling what she felt, living what she lived! That's what I tell myself, at least. The reality is that I'm safe at home in my bathtub and can get out anytime I want. In order to really experience what Eliza experienced, I'd have to enter a situation in which I also feel trapped.

I'm fascinated by writers who engage experientially in research. I admire their commitment and worry for their safety. I think they're profoundly courageous and batshit crazy. Whenever I bring this up, someone asks if I'm talking about Hunter S. Thompson—the drugs, the Hell's Angels—but my personal case-in-point is far less well known. In fact, I have no idea if he ever published anything.

Again, the gist: I was at a techno club—black lights, strobe lights, relentless beat—and some guy asked if he could buy me a drink. I was a first-year philosophy major (don't ask) with a newly purchased fake ID. It was my first time in a real grown-up bar. I ordered an Amaretto Stone Sour, and as I took the first sip, he asked if he could be my slave for a week.

I asked him to please repeat the question.

"Can I be your slave?" he said, and then, in response to the look on my face, "I'm a writer. I'm writing a collection of essays. In each one I'm someone's slave for a week, and I write about what they make me do."

"What do they make you do?" I asked—and yes, I know, I was gullible as all hell, and probably he was lying through his teeth, but who cared. It was the best, craziest, most awful story my eighteen-year-old self had ever heard. One woman prostituted him to her gay friends and kept the money. Another made him clean her house wearing only a saddle. A suburban couple filmed him setting himself on fire. "They made me pour lighter fluid in my hair," he said, "like it was shampoo or something."

"Why do you do all this stuff?" I asked, aghast. "Why not just imagine it?"

"You mean like *fiction*?" he said, like it was a bad word. "People don't want fiction. They want the truth—the blood and guts and piss and shit."

I didn't have the wherewithal to tell him how, for me, fiction is truth. I hadn't yet lived enough, read enough, or dealt with enough writers in bars to be able to explain how a story—when it's done right—can help you find yourself in others, share realities that can't possibly be real, and show a person or people a world that you never before imagined. Blood and guts and piss and shit? Sure, but joy and courage and hope and understanding, too.

The kicker is the *when it's done right.*

Which is why I was sitting in the fucking bathtub.

•

In the third hour, the water has drained below my hips, and my knuckles and the soles of my feet are cracked like spider-webbed glass. My dad is a fisherman in Alaska now, and I think of the dead fish he pulls from the water, bloated and eerie blue. I think of all he taught me about appropriate wilderness behavior back when I was growing up in Michigan: camping and hunter safety and taking the canoe over waterfalls on the Shiawasee River. If he saw me now, sitting in this icy water for no discernible reason, he'd think I'd lost it entirely.

"It's for a story," I'd tell him.

He'd try hard to be sensitive; he's a big reader. Although one time he got pissed at Tom Wolfe for making a character go quail hunting with buckshot. "Does it have to be five hours?" he'd ask, rational and reasonable. "Can it maybe happen quicker?"

Could it? I thought of when the Eliza story actually happened to me, some two decades ago around my sixteenth birthday. The day was so beautiful, the water warm. I floated on my back, listening to my own breath underwater—in and out, in and out— and then suddenly they were there. First, just one, and then he called for the rest: six, maybe? Seven? They all stood at the edge of jagged rock, looking down at me, trapped in a fishbowl below them. Instinctively, I locked myself into a ball and moved towards shallow water—low enough so I could stand, but still high enough to shield how naked I was. God, the shame! When you're sixteen! I've had so many relationships with my body; it's been a source of power, hatred, pride, life, but that day in the quarry was the first time I'd felt shame.

How much time passed that day? Truly, I don't remember. It could have been five minutes; it could have been five hours.

"Stand up," they yelled. "We just want to see!"

"Stand up. We're not gonna do anything to you!"

"Are you fucking deaf? Stand up!"

But I didn't. I was frozen. I was terrified. I was ashamed. It was so much bigger than five minutes.

But five hours?

After five hours, I'd surely remember the water growing cold. My feet, split and cracked. My skin, blue like fish. Wouldn't I remember?

•

In the fourth hour, I panic. The tub is nearly drained and my face is puffy. My hands are swollen, my body heavy like a wet blanket. I'm remembering bits and pieces of biology lectures, articles from *Scientific American*, and things Dad said on the boat out in the ocean, where being smart might mean your life. What had he said about hypothermia? Didn't I read something about trench foot? Muscle atrophy—what was that? And didn't David Blaine do this, and his skin like peeled off?

This is stupid, I decide. Even for me, and I've done some stupid shit; I did acid one time at the opera. And now I'm counting down the minutes, shivering in an empty bathtub? A bathtub! It's not even the right kind of water! Eliza's quarry is full of organisms! Minerals! The setting sun changes the water temperature! She is thirteen-years-old; I am thirty-five, and sixteen, too. All of us were in that quarry. The story changes with every telling, and—like Tim O'Brien being unable to remember the smell of the mud in Vietnam—I can't for the life of me remember what happened to my skin that day in the quarry.

•

By the fifth hour, I've given up. I'm on the couch, wrapped in a blanket. My body is too heavy, my head too light. I feel better after the first hot water and bourbon. Better after the second. And the third.

After a while, I get my laptop and Google "Being underwater for long periods of time."

THE WALLS WOULD
BE RUBBLE

I JUST PEED ON THE STICK, and now I have to wait three minutes. It's seven twenty-five and fourteen seconds and, according to the instructions on the box, in three minutes either a plus sign or a minus sign will appear in the little window, which means by seven-twenty *eight* and fourteen seconds, I'll know if my entire life just changed.

Funny how time plays tricks on you; one second I'm a freshman at a nice East Coast university with my nice Midwestern boyfriend, and then—

I get a scholarship to study in Italy, and suddenly I'm here in Florence, meeting people from all over the world, looking at art that's a million years old until—

I get back to the pensione late one night, and there's the nice Midwestern boyfriend, sitting on the steps with a backpack and a flower. "I crossed the ocean for you," he said. It was really, really perfect.

Except a few months later, I'm sitting in a bathroom stall in an eight-dollar-a-night hostel; the kind with fifty bunk beds in a single room and a bathroom like some high school gym: row of sinks, row of showers, row of stalls. I locked myself in the last one, up against the wall, and peed on the stick.

Now all there is to do is wait.

Seven twenty-six and five seconds.

Seven twenty-six and ten seconds.

It smells in here—*fifteen.* The florescent lights are buzzing—*twenty.* From the hall, I can hear voices, but I don't recognize the language—*twenty-five, twenty-six, twenty-seven, twenty-eight*—and never in my life have I felt this alone.

Seven twenty-six and thirty seconds.

I don't even know how to find an English-speaking doctor—*forty, forty-one, forty-two*—let alone get it taken care of—*forty-four, forty-five, forty-six.* Can you even do that in a Catholic country?

And I realize that keeping it never once entered my head.

Seven twenty-seven.

I got the pregnancy test from Janine, this girl from class who'd brought a ten-pack in her suitcase. "It's *Italy,*" she'd said. "All they *do* in Italy is have sex!" She's the one who told me to send my nice Midwestern boyfriend home, back across the ocean, so I'd be free to Enjoy The Culture. But I couldn't. I love him. I'm eighteen. The world is at my feet, a red carpet spread out before me—*seven twenty-seven and eight seconds, nine seconds, ten, eleven.*

When I told the nice Midwestern boyfriend I was late, he said, "For what?"

When I said, "*Late,* late," he didn't say anything.

Then, he got up and, without looking at me, went into the

bathroom and turned on the shower. "Aren't we going to talk?" I said, following. He was standing fully dressed under the faucet. He hadn't pulled the curtain, so water was spraying everywhere. His eyes were shut tight, his clothes hung drenched and heavy, pulling him down like he was sinking. And I realized then that if he couldn't hold himself up, how was he ever going to hold onto me?

I get it, though. He never signed up for this.

Neither had I.

Seven twenty-eight.

I left the apartment, wandering the dark cobblestone streets 'til I found this hostel with its hidden bathroom stall, horrible florescent lights, no familiar faces—*ten, nine, eight*—and I peed on the stick—*seven, six*—I am so, so stupid—*five, four—Please,* I think. *Please, please please—three, two—*

And all that's left to do is look.

A few years ago, an old friend from Alaska came to visit me in Chicago, and we started talking about abortion. Neither of us meant to go there. My friend—let's call her Kelly—said something about how her new governor was a woman, and I was all impressed.

"Do you like her?" I asked, which in retrospect, was the exact moment of my downfall, 'cause Kelly said, "Yes," and I said, "Why?" and she wrapped her fingers around the stem of her wine glass and said, "Because she's pro-life."

We were at a swanky Italian place downtown. It was midsummer—a lovely, decadent afternoon with people strolling lazily down the sidewalk—so we sat outside. We were supposed to be reconnecting over Chianti and Caprese salad, but instead we were gripping the dishware, suddenly on the defense and poised for a fight.

I know politics is a dicey subject for anyone's lunchtime conversation, but Kelly and I are especially volatile. Maybe you have a friend like that?

On one side of the table, you've got me: Twenty-six at the time, with ripped jeans, ponytails, and thick-rimmed glasses I didn't really need. I'd lived in five cities in three different countries. I was a college teacher, a registered Democrat in a very Blue state, and not quite atheist but leaning that way. Also, it's important to note: I was a hothead. Probably still am, but I like to think I've learned a little self-control. In fact, I probably learned it from this very conversation.

On the other side of the table, we've got Kelly: Also in her late-twenties, in an oversized T-shirt, clogs, and thick-rimmed glasses she really does need. She's lived her whole life in rural Alaska. Mother of two, a registered Republican in a very Red state (we're talking fire engine red; like, imagine a stop sign. That's Alaska). Also, it's important to note: her faith is the forefront of her life. It's given her joy, comfort, and the strength to slay some pretty profound fucking dragons, which is something I've always respected and even, at times, envied.

As you might imagine, we can get into it, yelling ourselves hoarse over gun control, oil, No Child Left Behind, tax reform, her church, and my lack of it. And to Kelly's credit, I've always walked away having learned something. She's smart. She listens. I like fighting with her.

But my body is not something I should have to fight about.

"Pro-life," she said that day at Gratzi's.

And I said, "Oh."

We sat there.

Half of me hoped she'd press it. Like, *Come on. Give me a reason to erupt, volcano-like, spilling anger and guilt and reality all over this starched-white tablecloth.*

But the other half? *Please drop it,* I thought. *Please.*

She didn't.

"I believe," she said, her words slow and cautious, 'cause maybe what she wanted to say was: Life begins at conception; that child's heart, however weak, is beating.

She didn't say that. She said, "I believe all life is precious."

I wanted to say how pro-choice doesn't mean anti-life; how, for me, it's about choosing a better life, one where that child is wanted.

But I didn't say that. I said, "I believe it's precious, too."

We stared at each other across the plates and napkins and bowls of pasta—so close, yet miles and miles and miles away. I thought of all she'd been through: losing her mother to a long, slow battle with cancer; her father passing not long after; several heart-wrenching miscarriages. For her, it's just so simple: *Life is precious. The end.*

For me, it's: *Life is precious. The beginning.*

I just peed on the stick, and now I have to wait three minutes.

It's ten thirty-five and twenty seconds, so by ten thirty-eight and twenty seconds—I'll know. I shouldn't be getting all excited because my husband and I have only been trying a couple months. But, this morning, I had this *feeling.* I was going to meet my friend Amy at Uncommon Ground, and something made me pull over at Walgreens and buy the three-pack of Fact Plus tests. What was that something, you ask? I don't know. Hormones?

Magic? Jesus Christ, Our Lord? Whatever—I get to the coffee shop, tell Amy to order me a Chai, be right back, gotta pee, and here I am.

Ten thirty-six.

Have you ever been in the bathroom at Uncommon Ground? It's nice. I mean, if you ever have to wait out a pregnancy test, I highly recommend it: small, private, stars painted on the ceiling; mosaic trees built into the wall, like you're in a forest—*ten thirty-six and thirty seconds, ten thirty-six and thirty-one seconds.* But, okay, realistically, I can't be pregnant. We haven't even been trying! I'm not counting days on the calendar, I don't have a little watch that lights up when you ovulate, I never showed up at my husband's office and made him have sex with me in a conference room. Okay, fine, I did do that. Also, the freight elevator, his uncle's swimming pool, and that schkeevy motel in Texas—but all that was for fun. We're not trying to get pregnant!

We're just not not trying.

We're not not trying really hard.

Ten thirty-seven and ten seconds. Eleven seconds. Twelve.

"Not not is a double negative," my friend Jeff told me, and I was all *Huh?* 'cause I'm not much with the grammar. "To not not try is the same as trying," he said. We were out with some friends, and I was drinking 7-Up, so everyone was all OHMY-GOD YOU'RE NOT DRINKING YOU MUST BE PREGNANT, and I was like, "No, I just don't feel like drinking," and they're all HAHA-HAHA— *yeah.*

"Are you trying?" Jeff asked later, and I said no, 'cause, really, we haven't been. Unless you count all the discussions, the planning, saving money, prenatal vitamins, going off the pill, and having all sorts of sex all the time—which, okay, fine, it's trying.

I just don't want to say it out loud.

I don't want to jinx it.

Ten thirty-eight.

Because, this kid... I want him more than anything—*ten, nine, eight*—I could explode this bathroom with the sheer power of my brain—*seven, six*—the walls would be rubble, the pipes would burst and, in the end, there's only me, sitting in a pile of dust with the stick in my hand—*five, four. Please*, I think. *Please, please please—three, two—*

And all that's left to do is look.

MY DAUGHTER CAN READ JUST FINE

WHEN I WAS IN THIRD GRADE, maybe fourth, my teacher called in my mother to tell her I couldn't read. My memory of this moment is fits and spurts: I remember mom and I sitting in little-kid desks across from the teacher in her ginormous teacher's desk. I remember being scared I was in trouble; your mom gets called in, that means you screwed up, right? I remember the classroom was on the second floor, with windows overlooking the playground, and there were seesaws shaped like sea animals. My mom has since filled in the blanks for much of what happened: apparently, there were these workbooks we were supposed to read, with stories about frogs and cats and stuff, and we had to answer multiple choice worksheets:

A. The frog is happy.

B. The frog is sad.

C. The frog is thinking.

My teacher showed my mother my worksheets. All the multiple choice questions were wrong—big red X's through the A's and B's and C's.

I *do* remember this next part: my mother looked at me and smiled. What my teacher didn't know was that my mom has a master's degree in early childhood education and was then designing a K-5 Gifted and Talented program for Washtenaw County. You want to hear a thing or two about kids and reading? Take my mom out for a beer. But, more important than that, I was *her kid*; you don't need a master's degree to be an expert in your own child.

I remember she held up the workbook with the frog story and asked, "Megan. Did you read this?" I shook my head no. Mom tapped the stack of workbooks on the teacher's desk, a semester's worth of frog stories, and asked, "Did you read *any* of these?" Again, I shook my head. "What were you reading instead?" I went to my desk, got the dog-eared copy of *Little Women*, and brought it back to my mother. She thumbed through its pages and, somewhere around page 300, asked me to tell her about it. I remember my fear of the teacher, the classroom, the workbooks—all of it fell away as I told my mom about how Jo didn't want to get married, how the girls all helped that family at Christmas, and how Beth died (to this day, that scene makes me cry). I *loved* that book, especially because it was about sisters; I wanted sisters. In retrospect, the March girls kind of were my sisters. I profoundly believe in the relationships we have with fictional characters—what they teach us, how they help us grow and see the world and see ourselves.

Anyhow, I remember my mother patted me on the shoulder. Then she turned and, very slowly, very purposefully, gave my teacher a *look*. I will never forget that look for as long as I live. It held fury and pride and a rapidly brewing thunderstorm of words. Heavy words. Dangerous ones. Over the years, I've been grateful that, no matter how much stupid shit I pulled, my mother never looked at *me* with *that* look. And it wasn't until I became a parent that I truly understood its magnitude.

Three decades later, as a teacher myself, I think about that teacher making such a snap judgment about my reading ability. Her assessment could have changed my life completely; at worst, I could've been held back, and at—not best; no, a different *kind* of worst—I was being labeled: *Can't Read.* Granted, labels can be helpful, offering much-needed support for a myriad of challenges kids are up against, but they also have a lasting impact on a kid's psyche and should be treated with care. Can I tell you how many college students come to my classes with horror stories of What Teachers Told Them? *You can't read, you can't write, you're dumb, you're bad.* And then teachers tell parents, and sometimes parents believe it because teachers are the experts, right? And the parents—they're *tired*, overworked; believe me, I'm a parent. I know tired and overworked.

But I'm also a teacher. I know tired and overstuffed classrooms. I know too many students and too much student work. I know too many hours and not enough to pay my mortgage. And how do you manage it all? Do you take shortcuts? And what might those shortcuts do to the student in the long run? What I'm trying to say here is that my teacher screwed up, yes, but to say this is entirely her fault is a whole other systematic problem that needs to be addressed. It's not as easy as, "Some teachers are good and some are bad, and let's make these oversimplified judgments by testing students on reading comprehension when maybe, just maybe, kids are filling out those multiple choice questions without even reading about the fucking frog!"

Imagine where my life might have gone had my mother not been the woman she is—my advocate, my watchdog, my *parent.* And FYI, I'd like to include the idea of "significant adult" in this discussion because I've known many awesome kids raised by aunts, grandparents, foster parents, friends, or any number of amazing, selfless people who want to make this world a better place for their kid and everyone else's, too.

I write stories because I love reading, and I love reading because my mother put books in my hands, read them with me, asked me what I thought about them, listened as I told her, and gave me other books to read based on my replies. She did this for years—she *still* does it—so imagine, after all of *that*, being told by some teacher who barely knew me that I couldn't read? I'm not a religious person, but Lord Almighty! What would you have done, sitting in that little-kid desk as someone told you something untrue about your very own child?

My mom is a dignified lady. I try very hard to follow her example, and more often than not, I fail. I tend to turn red, fly off the handle, and let the words out of my mouth before thinking them through. Over the years, I've learned that this approach doesn't do anyone any good, and there've been many times when, on the edge of exploding all over the place, I've summoned up the memory of my mother on that day. She smoothed her skirt over her knees. She smiled. Then she said, "As you can see, my daughter can read just fine." My teacher must have said something here. Or, maybe she just took off her foot and stuck it in her mouth? I don't remember. What I *do* remember is my mother calmly explaining, in a voice that offered no room for discussion—a voice not unlike the Book of Genesis—that this teacher would no longer have anything to do with my English education. I would come to class every day and do math and science and social studies with everyone else, but when the rest of the class did their reading and their workbooks, I would be doing assignments that she—*my mother*—would send to school. Then she—*my mother*—would grade those assignments, and she—*my mother*—would share that grade with her—the teacher—and if there were any questions about all of this, perhaps they should set up an appointment with the Superintendent of Schools?

For the rest of the year, when everyone else would read about frogs and fill out their multiple choice, I would read the books my mother gave me: *Charlotte's Web*; *The Great Gilly Hopkins*; *Bridge to Terabithia*; *Where the Red Fern Grows*; *Ramona Quimby*; *A Wrinkle in Time*; *Jennifer, Hecate, MacBeth, William McKinley and Me, Elizabeth*; *The Egypt Game*; *A Cricket in Times Square*; *Mrs. Frisby and the Rats of NIHM*; *Jacob Two-two and the Hooded Fang*; *The Pushcart War*; *Island of the Blue Dolphins*; and on and on. I had lots of spiral-bound notebooks full of questions, and not multiple choice questions, but questions—ones I had to think through and explain; ones that brought me to new questions that I had to think through, explain, and often talk about with my mom and dad. And, look at that! Now we're talking about the world!

Suddenly, reading means this whole other thing to me: I'm not just *watching* the characters of Karana and Rontu and Rontu-Aru running around on the island of blue dolphins, I'm imagining myself there with them. I'm seeing it all from their point of view, and for a little girl growing up in small-town Southeast Michigan, seeing the world through the eyes of a little girl growing up in Ghalas-at on San Nicolas Island was a *gift*. What a profound introduction to literature! I remember reading about Karana and wondering why the things she does after her father and brother die, things like hunting and fishing, were traditionally only tasks for men. My dad took me hunting and fishing, and I was a girl! I look back and laugh at this childhood outrage, but I'm grateful for it, too. There I am, eight years old, starting to think over some pretty fucking big truths. Here's another truth: I didn't know what foster care was, or that some children didn't have parents, until I read *The Great Gilly Hopkins*. The kind of kid I was back then lived in a sort of bubble: your own home and neighborhood and school. I remember that book changing the way I thought about gratitude and survival and perseverance, and it started a dialogue about privilege that I'm still, to this day, trying to work through and learn about. I've had that experience with a lot of books over the past twenty years. Through reading, I learn about points of view that are different than my own. It starts the dialogue. It opens my eyes to things I haven't seen before. It inspires me to share this gift with others.

That's why I write.

That's why I teach writing.

It's how I was taught.

JUGGLE WHAT?

What is the rudest question you can ask a woman? "How old are you?"
"What do you weigh?" "When you and your twin sister are alone with
Mr. Hefner, do you have to pretend to be lesbians?" No, the worst
question is "How do you juggle it all?" —Tina Fey

I AM OFTEN ASKED how I juggle it all. This can mean many things, depending on who's asking: How do I juggle being a writer and a mom, a teacher and a mom, a working mom, and a mom, period?[1] Submitting my writing, marketing my writing, performing my writing, writing? Teaching students, teaching teachers to teach students, learning from these teachers and students and writers and moms—'cause, really, what the hell do I know?

I am often asked how I juggle it all, and the truth is: I'm lucky. My husband is a total hands-on dad and 100% supportive of my work. He even taught our three-year-old to ask, when I get home at the end of the day, "How'd the writing go, Mommy?"[2]

I am often asked how I juggle it all, and the truth is: I'm lucky. My kid is spectacular in a thousand ways that, like any parent, I could go on about forever,[3] but what's pertinent here is that he's a great sleeper. Eleven hours per night and a two-hour nap.

Everything I've written since he was born has happened during these two hours. He conks out and I get to work. There are dishes and toys and laundry everywhere; a hundred new emails marked priority; the house is on fire, burning to the ground as I type; and none of it matters. These are my two hours. I am able to exist as an individual independent of my role as a mother because of them. I guard them. They are precious, the last canteen in a barren desert.

Here's how I used to write: My workspace had to be clean, notes organized, a certain kind of coffee, *what music would best suit my mood?* I'd read a little, stare at the wall, go to the kitchen for more coffee, and—*Whoa, look at how gross the oven is, better clean it,* and—*Shit. The fridge is nasty, too. And the floor.* And of course, the kitchen floor is connected to the rest of floor, and by the time the whole apartment is spotless, I've given up on writing for the day because I don't "feel inspired."

Fuck waiting for it.

Sit down and make it happen.

I am often asked how I juggle it all, and what I say is, "It's how you use the time you've got."

Do I sound like I know what I'm doing? It's not altogether true. I feel a bit fragile about my writing, actually. Here are some reasons why:

1. Sometimes, I can't write during those two hours because I have to be at work.

2. Sometimes, I can't write during those two hours because I have to nap.

3. Sometimes, I can't write during those two hours because

my brain hurts and the only way to fix it is to watch Jack Bauer on Netflix.

4. Sometimes, when I can write during those two hours, I don't know what to work on. A short story? This essay? A blog post, or two, or five,? That interview that was due last week? My journal? What I want to work on is my novel, but to tackle something so big with only two little hours... it just seems impossible.

5. I'm ashamed to admit that; my students might be reading this.

6. What I want to work on is my novel. I walk around thinking about it, and sometimes I run into walls or miss my L stop. I've written short stories for a decade, but this—there are so many characters! Recently, I was talking through some dialogue to keep them all straight in my mind, and my son looked up from his Legos and said, "Mommy, are you talking to yourself?

7. I thought of the scene in *The Hours* when Virginia Woolf is going insane, and her niece asks why she's talking to herself, and her sister Vanessa is all, "It's okay, honey. Aunt Virginia's a writer."

8. "Yes," I said to my three-year-old. "I'm talking to myself."

9. He hugged me. Have you ever been hugged by a three-year-old? It's the greatest feeling in the history of the universe.

10. He pulled free of the hug and put both little hands on my cheeks. "You don't have to talk to yourself, Mommy," he said. "You can talk to me!"

I try to juggle it all. I have a very complex system of color-coded Google calendars: CALEB, CHRISTOPHER, WRITING, TEACH-

ING, CITE, 2ND STORY, and LIFE (for example: "Go to the dentist", "Buy groceries"). In fact, I just added a new one! It's called SELF-PRESERVATION.

This week, there are three things scheduled under SELF-PRESERVATION: Murakami's *IQ84*, yoga class, and *Have a Good Cry*.

Recently, when complaining to my friend Amanda about how I can't juggle it all, I started to cry. We were driving somewhere with my son in the backseat. I went on and on about the pressure, the exhaustion, the mortgage, how I'd cut off my left arm for an uninterrupted week to write. "... And to top it all off, fucking Halloween is coming! When am I going to find him a costume!? Let alone fucking make one! Some mothers go to JoAnn Fabric and get the patterns and FUCKING MAKE JIMMY INTO A PENGUIN. WHO HAS THAT KIND OF TIME!?"

FYI: I didn't really swear in front of my son.

That said, I wanted to.

Sometimes, it's all too much.

Amanda listened to me explode all over the car and then, calmly, she got out her cell phone and turned to the back seat. "Caleb," she said, dialing. "What do you want to be for Halloween?"

"Light-up Batman!" he said, which made me cry harder 'cause it's so totally adorable. And while I sat there unable to control my gulpy, gaspy sobs—my sweet little boy asking if I was okay and could he please unbuckle his car seat and come up front to hug me—my friend Amanda got on the phone and ordered a Batman costume. Size 5T.

"And if it could light up somehow, that be great." Then she hung up, looked at me and said, "What else?"

I am often asked how I juggle it all, and the truth is: it takes a village. As I type these words, my son is with his Uncle Jeff. Jeff is a bartender at a fancy French place and wants his god-son to be educated in high-end cuisine. To that end, they take a monthly tour of Chicago's best gastropubs. My son comes home stuffed and excited, toddler-talking a mile a minute about riette, cornichons, and haricot vert, and I get new pages of my novel. Maybe an essay or two.

Jeff is also a writer. He understands my need to get the words out of my head and on to the page. He knows it makes me... calmer.

It is rare, if ever, that I feel calm. I drop my son off at school and am floored by all the mothers, so put-together, so sophisticated. I am exhausted from teaching 'til ten the night before. I have probably, recently, spilled juice on myself. A good day is when we leave the house on time with the necessary stuff: Caleb's backpack, and my backpack, and student work, and books, and my computer, and keys, and the avocado plant for Show'n'Share, and coffee, and *did I walk the dog? Did I make my deadline? Did I write down the idea I had in the middle of the night about how to transition between chapters 3 and 4 of my novel? It was a great fucking idea!* WHAT WAS IT!? We get everything in the car, Caleb's strapped in, I'm strapped in—and then I just sit there. I breathe. It's 8 a.m. The day hasn't even started, but already, I look around for applause.

Recently, when complaining to a friend about how I couldn't juggle it all, a woman I'd never met leaned over from the next table and said, "Tina Fey has an essay about parenting in this week's *New Yorker*. Maybe you should read it."

I love Tina Fey. I have always loved Tina Fey. She's on my

list—the one my husband and I made, prior to getting married—of people we'd be allowed to cheat with if ever the situation presented itself (Tina Fey, Idris Elba, and PJ Harvey from the "Rid Of Me" video circa November 2007). I admire her humor, the doors she's opening for women in Hollywood and hopefully this country—life follows art, right? Most importantly, I'm grateful for her honesty about how being a working mom is hard even when you have help. See how she does that? Admits having help, so legions of us working moms don't compare ourselves to the impossible model of Tina Fey producing a television show, writing a bestseller, dressing up in designer duds, and fighting twenty times a day with a toddler about putting chocolate sauce on the broccoli?

How do I juggle it all?

I have help.

Dear my cousin Aaron: thank you for helping me take care of my son. Thank you for picking him up from school when my meetings ran late. Thank you for taking him to the park so I could finish that grant application. Thank you for reading him a story before bed on those nights I passed out on the couch at 6 p.m. Thank for appearing out of the clear blue sky the moment my family and I most needed you.

Did you hurt yourself on your fall from heaven?

Not gonna lie: when that woman—that stranger—told me that Tina Fey's essay could help with my parenting, I wanted to stick a fork in her eye. I was eating a very gooey Danish with a fork, and I imagined reaching across the table, plucking her eyeball right out of her face, and flinging it across the coffee shop.

Giving unsolicited advice is never a good idea.

Especially when it's about parenting.

I can't speak for anyone but myself, but I feel a bit fragile about my parenting. Here are some reasons why:

1. As a college writing teacher, I read a lot of My Mother Screwed Me Up Good stories.

2. There are so many My Mother Screwed Me Up Good stories, many of which feature women who are artists but stop making art when they have kids, and then blame the kids, and then the kids go to therapy and grow up and write books like *Running With Scissors.*

3. I didn't stop making art when I had a kid, nor have I stopped helping others make art, in part because I love my job, but also because I need it (Hi, Fannie Mae!). And no matter how fast I run, no matter how much I write, no matter how much permission I have to be a Working Mother in the Twenty-first Century, I still feel guilty. Last week I got an email from school about which parents would help the kids change into their Halloween costumes and which parents would buy juice. I had two meetings, a four-hour workshop, and an annual report due that day, so I bought the juice.

4. I am the mother who buys the juice.

5. I sat on the kitchen floor and cried about being the mother who buys the juice. I vowed to quit work immediately. We'd pay our mortgage somehow, right? And if not, who cares? We'll mail our house keys to the bank, pack up the dog, and go live in a cabin. Preferably one with a goat. I'll help my kid change into his Halloween costume every day, and we'll only drink milk. Never juice. Fuck juice.

6. This cry had not been scheduled on my SELF-PRESERVATION Google calendar.

7. My three-year-old came into the kitchen wanting to know why I was sad.

8. I said, "Because I bought juice."

9. He put both his little hands on my cheeks and said, "Mommy, I love juice!"

10. Then he said, "Can you be done now so we can play?"

I am often asked how I juggle it all, and the truth is this: I can sit there crying on the floor, or I can get up and build a super-ramp with my kid. I can worry about what and how and when I'm writing, or I can put my ass in the chair and do it already. It's how you use the time you've got.

In the end, there are these calm, lovely, perfect moments. Everything has slowed down. We're reading bedtime stories. We're coloring spaceships. We're making forts out of pillows, figuring out the impossible, puffy architecture. This month, we made enough to cover the bills so, for a few weeks at least, the weight of the world sits elsewhere, and for now it's just the three of us.

I think about how lucky I am. It's a big feeling—a thousand times bigger than my novel ever could be. It's so big that I almost stop breathing.

My whole life, there've been two things I've known for sure: I want to be a writer, and I want to be a mom. And now? People ask how I juggle it all, and what I want to say is, "Are you kidding? My life isn't a juggle."

It's a fucking gift.

Footnotes:

1. I'm using the word "Mom" here because that's what I am, but I think this applies to dads, too. And the aunts, grandparents, foster parents, and significant adults who are raising super-awesome kids that make this world a better place.

2. Rarely, if ever, is my husband asked how he juggles it all. I wonder why that is?

3. When I get mad because somebody parked in my parking spot, he says, "Mommy, you have to share." He says, "Mommy? My body needs to run now. Can we go somewhere for this?" He says, "My body is full of bones and meat and mus-kulls." He says, "Mommy-Ramen-aminal" for Mayor Rahm Emanuel. He says, "Will you be my friend? Friends are super cool." He says, "Can we listen to that M.I.A. song? M.I.A shakes my butt." He says, "You're the best Mommy I've ever had in my whole life ever," and a thousand other amazing things, a thousand times a day. For him, I want to be a better human being, a better writer, teacher, wife, and friend. For him, I want the world to be a better place. I think art can help make that happen. And someday—two decades into the future when he's finding himself as an adult—I want him to read my stories and be proud of me. Which means that now? I need to get to work.

WHO WANTS THE SHOT

I GOT MY FIRST GUN when I was fourteen: a Remington Express 12-gauge that I called Rhonda, after the Beach Boys song. I'd been out hunting with my dad a thousand times before—he tells a story about chasing rabbits with me in a toddler backpack—but this was the first time I'd held one, loaded one, lifted one, and felt its pull.

"Press the butt of the gun into your right shoulder," Dad instructed, his big arms over mine. "Then lift the barrel with your opposite hand." He'd tacked a poster of the Incredible Hulk to a tree about ten yards off our garage, and I shut my left eye and peered through the scope; it was like looking through the circle at the end of a toilet paper roll, except it had plus-sign in the middle. My job was to plant that plus sign right between the Hulk's eyes.

I held Rhonda steady and looked for my shot: circle of grass, circle of sky, circle of Hulk.

"Got it," I said, flipping off the safety. The Hulk's eyes and nose were clenched into a triangle. That triangle was my entire adolescent universe. "Wait for your moment," Dad whispered, and I felt my heartbeat in my throat. "You'll know if you want the shot."

After a few months of practice, once the Hulk's face was sufficiently shredded and the gun's pull didn't knock me off my feet, Dad took me out bird hunting. We were in one of a thousand fields in Southeast Michigan—memory is blurry at best, but I can still see the knee-high, brittle grass spread around me like a football field. And there, in the middle, is my dad in all camouflage. I wore camouflage, too, and pigtails under a Detroit Tigers cap. I was so proud, so excited, so big-boy tough out there with my dad. And then, after a few minutes, bored out of my skull.

Ninety percent of hunting is waiting around, and I didn't have it in me. Not then, not now. "Can we go home yet?" I whined, and suddenly, Dad held out his arm. This meant stop, so I froze. Dad was listening, head cocked to the side, so I cocked mine and listened, too: wind. More wind. Our dog, Duchess, a springer spaniel with birds in her blood, was frozen, nose in the air. And then, right in front of us from somewhere in the underbrush, a barely perceptible crunch of grass; immediately, Dad was on the move, creeping in a wide arc around whatever it was so he could rush it from behind and scare it back towards me. In the meantime, I pulled Rhonda to my shoulder and counted down from ten. Nine. Eight. Seven. Six, and then everything happened at once: the underbrush exploded, there were feathers and flapping wings, and not five feet in front me, a pheasant burst into the sky. I tilted Rhonda back to keep it in my sights—circle of tree, circle of sky, circle of bird. It was so beautiful, so free. All that practice with the Hulk poster, and I somehow hadn't expected the target to, like, move. I pulled my head back, lowered Rhonda forever to my side, and watched that bird climb the sky.

"You'll know if you want the shot," Dad had said, and obviously, I didn't. I didn't want to kill it. What I wanted was for my dad to be proud of me, to be part of his world, to give him something he could stuff and mount on the wall next to the Dall sheep head he'd brought back from Alaska. He loved Alaska—living there was his dream—and after I took off for college, he took off to an island in the Gulf. He built a salmon fishing boat in his backyard. He spent weeks at a time tracking moose in the mountains.

Have you ever seen your parents happy?

It's the greatest thing in the goddamn universe.

When I was twenty-eight, I took my boyfriend Christopher to Alaska to meet my father. For the record: this was the first time I'd ever introduced a guy to my dad, mostly because he was (and is) my hero, but also because when I'd started high school he wrote up a document titled "APPLICATION TO DATE MY DAUGHTER." It had questions like:

Do you now or ever intend to get a tattoo?

Which of the following would indicate a damaged carburetor?

What is the significance of the beans in chapt. 7 of Thoreau's *Walden*?

He said it was a joke, but I was never really sure, and I'd give copies to guys I was dating to see how they'd react. Most of them laughed, but Christopher studied the questions carefully before asking, "Is it okay if I type my answers on separate paper and then attach them to the original?"

I booked tickets the next day.

To get to my dad's, you fly commercial to Anchorage and then take a jet to Kodiak. From the sky, it's green and lush—the Emerald Isle, they call it—but once you hit the ground, you can't see your own shoes through the fog. Dad was waiting on the tarmac when we landed; his arms were crossed, brows raised, head-to-toe in camo. Even *I* was intimidated.

"Dad," I said—there was weight to this moment, a plot point of my history—"This is Christopher." We both turned to him; he was shivering in khakis and a Ben Sherman sweater, which is a perfectly logical thing to wear when meeting the parents, but sort of ridiculous if you're meeting the parents in Alaska in December. They did the *Hello* and the *Nice to meet you*, then Dad looked at Christopher's Chuck Taylors and asked, "Did you bring any boots?"

Christopher glanced at me. "Uhm—"

"I've got extras at home," Dad said. "We can swing by and grab 'em after we get your license."

"My license?"

"Can't hunt without a license."

Christopher is a web designer. He can climb into the brain of your computer and make it speak fifteen languages. He's a genius and a romantic, and he'll kick your ass at bowling. But guns?

"You don't have to do this," I told him, back at the house. He was decked out in my dad's extra camo, except Christopher is six-five, so my dad's pants hit his shins.

"I *do* have to," he said. "More than anything I've ever done in my life."

I've heard him tell this story a thousand times, and it's not hard to imagine how it happened: Christopher, hiking through knee-high snow in the mid-afternoon darkness, trying desperately to keep up with his girlfriend's sixty-year-old father. It's cold out there—not ice-cold like mainland Alaska, but wet-cold from the island currents, so your bones soak instead of freeze. Christopher, in too-small boots, does his best to ignore it as the hours pass until finally, *finally* they arrive at a pile of underbrush that Dad intuitively recognizes as the ideal hiding place.

"You stand here," he tells Christopher, "and I'm going to go to the other side and scare out all the rabbits."

Christopher stops. "*All* the rabbits?"

"Yes, they'll run straight at you, and what you do then is you shoot them."

"Shoot them," Christopher repeats.

"Right."

Christopher considers this. "Where are you in relation to the rabbits?"

"Behind them," says my dad.

"You want me to shoot the rabbits, but you're behind the rabbits?"

"That's right."

"Okay." Christopher nods, working up the nerve to ask the obvious: "What if I shoot you?"

My dad thinks this over. "Yeah, don't do that," he says, and with those word of wisdom, he crouches down and disappears into the underbrush—same as he did with me and the pheasant so many years ago. Christopher stands there, his very first gun pressed into his shoulder, and after ten agonizingly silent minutes, he hears it: Barking. Barking and growling. A rabid dog, maybe? Something violent, with really big teeth, and it's getting louder, louder. The underbrush before him starts quivering, and at the same time, he realizes that the barking isn't coming from a dog; it's coming from my father pretending to be a dog. The line of brush before him explodes with rabbits. "You know that scene in Bambi?" Christopher told me later, "When the forest is on fire and all the animals are running away? It was like that." And what do you do? There's no time to think, only to act: circle of snow, circle of grass, circle of rabbit—BAM—another circle of rabbit—BAM—another—BAM—another—BAM—another—BAM— and when Christopher pulls back from the scope, there's a dead rabbit lying at his feet.

"You'll know if you want the shot," Dad always said, and obviously, Christopher wanted it. He wanted to impress my dad, to be a part of our family, to live something different than his day job and computer screens. We got married not long after that rabbit hunt, and every October, Christopher goes deer hunting with my dad and his brothers in Northwest Michigan.

No guns, though.

Bows.

A few years ago, my dad called me up in Chicago, and the first thing he said was, "Now don't panic," which, for the record, was not a good way to start the conversation because *of course I'm going to panic.* Not to mention, I'd recently had a baby and was hormonal and sleep-deprived and slightly insane.

"Did you get attacked by a shark?" I said. I'd been up all night feeding the baby and watching Animal Planet. "I just watched this episode where—"

Dad cut me off: "I didn't get attacked by a shark," he said, as though it was the stupidest thing he'd ever heard. "I got attacked by a bear."

Here's what happened: Dad and his brother Chuck were

tracking a moose, chasing its trail for over a week before cornering it in a brushfield between three sides of a mountain. They froze—they waited—ten, nine, eight—and the brush, almost imperceptibly, shook. Dad and Chuck have been hunting together since they were kids; they don't need words anymore. *You go around,* said my dad, with hands. *I'll stay here and wait for it.* Chuck nodded, sliding out of his pack and creeping around the brush, where he'd then scare the moose towards my dad the same way Dad scared the rabbits toward Christopher and the pheasant toward me.

"I pulled up the rifle," Dad said, and I waited, still terrified by the "Don't panic." "I could hear my own heartbeat it was so quiet," he said, "and then—" As he talked, I shut my eyes and saw the whole scene: Chuck yelling and barking and running towards the brush; the moose inside—panicking, thrashing, running—with its giant body cutting through the trees and gnarled vine and bursting forth towards that non-existent fourth wall—the only way out—and the only thing standing between it and its freedom was my dad.

Except it wasn't a moose.

The average Kodiak Brown Bear weighs 1500 pounds. They are five feet tall with all four paws on the ground, and over ten feet tall standing on their back legs, which is what that mother bear did when she saw my dad. Imagine that for a second; ten feet is as tall as your ceiling. The bear is as tall as your ceiling. She is scared, she is pissed, and there, in front of her, is my dad. And she goes for him: fifty yards, thirty yards, ten. One swipe with those mammoth claws, and my father might cease to exist completely.

There is no time to think, only to react: circle of foot, circle of stomach, circle of head; the plus sign locked on that triangle between the bear's nose and eyes. For forty years, my dad prepared for this moment on rabbits, partridge, deer, caribou, Elk, moose; All them requiring singular, focused aim. BAM—and the bear hits the ground. She's got a bullet in her brain. Her mammoth body would fill up your whole living room.

"You'll know if you want the shot," and, obviously, my dad wanted it. He wanted to live, to give Rhonda to his grandson someday, to pin a poster of the Incredible Hulk to a tree and teach him everything he taught me—the patience to wait for what you want, the diligence to train your mind and body, the balls to chase something that seems impossible, the wisdom to choose your battles, and the strength to carry them through. "Press the butt of the gun into your right shoulder," he'll say. "Then lift the barrel with your opposite hand." I imagine my little boy—nine, ten years from now; he's holding Rhonda steady and peering through the scope like it's a toilet paper roll: circle of grass, circle of sky, circle of Hulk.

He'll wait for his moment.

He'll know if he wants the shot.

FELT LIKE SOMETHING

MY OVARY IS THE SIZE of a cherry tomato. A cell the size of a grain of rice grew into a tumor the size of a tangerine and sucked up my ovary. Like Pac-Man. That's how my doctor explained it: "Like Pac-Man." Later, on the operating table and under all sorts of anesthetic, I remember thinking, *Pac-Man, hahaha,* before passing out completely. When I came to, she told me the tumor could have killed me. 32 years old. 6-week-old baby. Dead by tangerine.

I am in awe of the power in little things. For example: a space nebula the size of a pin could crack a hole in our galaxy; my vote could change the direction of our entire country; the clitoris, when properly stimulated, can explode part of a woman's brain; and a tumor the size of a tangerine made me believe.

In *something.*

I'm still trying to figure out what that means. Am I talking about God? If so, I'm painfully aware that this could be a scene from *Eat Pray Love*: white woman in her thirties has life-altering experience and runs off in search of The Divine. The thing is, I don't know what the The Divine means. I left the church when I was a teenager because of politics, dated too many boys with dreadlocks to be comfortable with The Spirit, and, frankly... I'm *busy.* I have three jobs and a very active three-year-old. Nurturing a belief system is way too much of a time commitment. Problem is, you still need to call yourself something, so I'd just say Atheist and leave it at that.

When I was in high school, it was easy—a lifestyle choice, if you will. I was that especially ridiculous kind of geek who would cut class in order to go to the library. I'd read Nietzsche, Darwin, Dawkins, and all sorts of heady texts with titles like *The God Delusion* or *The Case against Christianity.* If you were stoned enough to get cornered by me at a party, I'd tell you all about the lead singer of Bad Religion getting a PhD in Zoology to "like, authenticate his lyrics"—seriously. You would have hated me. *I* hated me—but, at eighteen, don't we all? For shits and giggles, think back to yourself at that age. Why were you *like* that? Why did you believe what you believed? Why did you do the crazy things you did?

When I was eighteen, I went to see a psychic. Not because I believed in that stuff—Atheist, remember? I didn't believe in any stuff, but a girl who lived in my dorm asked me to go with her, and at the time I was so profoundly lonely that I'd have followed her to Siberia. This girl, I'll call her Nancy, was a bit of a stereotype: Birkenstocks—*check*—gauzy skirts—*check*—homemade beads of Femo clay—*check*—in her dreadlocks—*check check.* Also, she owned a drum. With which she went "drumming."

"I'm Nancy," she said the day we met, both of us lugging suit-cases down the hall, "but you can call me Persephone."

"No, I can't," I told her, 'cause if I did I'd asphyxiate on my own vomit. This was a phrase I used often at eighteen. I'd learned it from the movie *Heathers*. Have you seen *Heathers*? Winona Ryder plays this teenage girl who's all dark and angsty and murderous. I wanted to be Winona Ryder from *Heathers*, which means being friends with a girl like Nancy was enough to fuck me gently with a chainsaw.

For six months I endured her tarot cards and rain sticks, her Celtic runes and power crystals, her Ying Yang balls, dream catchers, hemp handbags, vegan cookies, wheatgrass, and altars to Shiva. But the absolute worst?—she had a dirty boyfriend. Not dirty like sex-dirty; dirty like the guy didn't believe in showering—something about natural human oils and masculine essence. Bottom line: he stank. Plus, he and Nancy had these ridiculous conversations like: "I love you Persephone." "I love you, Dawid"—he'd changed the *v* in David to a *w* 'cause of some Hebrew sun god, I think—and he'd say, "Not only do I love you, Persephone; you *are* love," and she'd say, "Because of you." Later, we'd discover there were lots of girls on campus whom not only did he love, they were love, and when Nancy learned that precious fact, she played Tori Amos on repeat and made an appointment with her psychic.

The place was called Spiritual Energy Readings. It was the *last* place I'd expect to connect with the greater power of the Universe. There were no candles. No bead curtains. No crystal balls or black cats or bloody chicken bones. Just a second floor storefront, not unlike the crack houses you see on *Law and Order*; a nasty carpet; a couple folding card tables; and a short, frizzy-haired woman named Contessa in a Led Zeppelin t-shirt and too much jewelry. Nancy took one look at her and burst into tears.

Contessa lit a Kool. "Ah," she said. "You have problem."

Nancy's puffy eyes widened. "I *do* have problem!"

Of course you have problem! I wanted to yell, but instead sat back and watched as Nancy crumbled into a lawn chair, dropped a twenty on the folding table, and spent the next half hour feeding this Orc of a woman all the information necessary to guess her whole life story.

"I miss him so much!"

"Ah, there is man."

"There *is* man!"

"And this man...he has left?"

"He *has* left!"

"There is other woman?"

There is seven other woman, I thought.

This went on for a long time. Contessa chain-smoked. She excused herself twice to answer the phone. She dealt a tarot deck like a Vegas blackjack dealer. Yet somehow, in the end, she made my friend feel better.

"I don't know how to thank you!" Nancy gushed, reaching into her free-trade purse for more cash. That's when Contessa lit another Kool and pointed at me.

"I don't think so," I said.

"You come," she said.

"*Hell* no," I said.

Looking back on it now, I wonder if she did have some kind of psychic gift, because she leaned back in her chair and said the one thing in the greater Universe that could've made me stay: "I see. You are afraid."

Had someone told Winona Ryder from *Heathers* that she was afraid, she'd have made them drink Draino. *Afraid? Me? No way/ no how!* I sat down in the lawn chair, took a Kool out of that pack, and used her Zippo to light it. I was going to say, "Bring it on, Contessa," but since I'd never smoked before, I just concentrated on not coughing.

She looked at my palms and gave me the usual: *Strong willed, travel far, give the world great things.* It was textbook-predictable. Just when I thought she'd bust out the *There is great curse on your family. Come back with thousand dollar and I lift it with innards of goat,* she switched to tarot cards. That's when things got weird.

She spread five out in front of me—cups, I think? Wands? Knight of Something I don't remember?—and she stared at them for a really, really long time.

Then she said, "Oh."

It's the single syllables that'll kill you: Your dentist says *Oops.* Your pregnancy test says *plus.* Your psychic says *Oh.*

"It could be nothing," she said.

But I looked at her face and knew it was something. I thought of Winona Ryder from *Heathers.* She wouldn't just sit there. She'd grab a switchblade out of her Doc Marten and slam it through this woman's hand. Then she'd say something very witty and obscene involving household appliances and get the hell out of there, down to the sidewalk and back into the world where free will reigned and fate didn't reside in some fifty-cent novelty store crystal. *Stand up,* I told myself. *Stand up and get out of here. You don't even believe in this stuff! You don't believe in any stuff!*—but the thing is?

Suddenly, I sorta did.

I imagined all the things that could be behind that *Oh.* Maybe I'd die tomorrow, maybe I'd kill someone tomorrow, maybe everyone would be killed tomorrow over something I said or did or thought. "Tell me," I said to Contessa, and it wasn't me being tough.

It was me being scared.

I don't remember exactly how she said it—something about my middle or my insides or my "lady parts"—but she did use the word *broken.* She said, "You are broken."

And for over a decade, I believed her.

I never *told* that to anyone, of course. I was an Atheist! Plus, how stupid would I have sounded, letting some storefront psychic get under my skin? So instead, I'd ignore the panicky feeling I'd have whenever I got a yearly check-up, or held a friends' new baby, or whispered with my husband about our Far Off In The Future Children. In fact, the first time I ever admitted my fears out loud was at a storytelling performance I gave at The Museum of Contemporary Art in Chicago. I was eight months pregnant at the time—cranky, swollen, and ready to kill for a pee that lasted longer than ten seconds—but safe from the possibility of Contessa's prediction. The gallery where I performed was wallpapered with eyeballs—these giant Andy Warhol pop art-looking things that made the audience feel like a thousand instead of a hundred. I stood at the microphone and told them about that crackhouse storefront, about Contessa with her frizzy hair and Led Zeppelin T-shirt. *Obviously she was a fraud because look at how pregnant I am! I'm so totally pregnant! Nothing broken here, thank you very much!* The crowd laughed, and I pushed harder: *It's not just Contessa,* I said, *it's all that mystical, magical hooha horseshit, power of the Universe, my ass!—God? I don't see any God!* It was like those movies where the ship is out in the middle of the ocean and there's some insane storm—thunder, lightning, waves crushing the deck to splinters—and in the middle of it all, the ship's captain hangs on the shredded sail, shaking his fist at the sky and telling God where to get off. That was me in the MCA: big ol' stomach, wall-to-wall eyeballs, yelling my head off at someone I didn't believe in.

A few weeks later, my son was born, and that—*that*—is when I should have believed. I built a human being *from scratch.* He was healthy, and awesome, and *hungry.* It wasn't possible for me to fully reflect on a possible spiritual awakening brought on by the miracle of giving birth! I was a 24-hour bottomless buffet! There wasn't room for thinking. I fed my kid. I slept. On a good day, I made the bed. I went to the store, the pediatrician, and—six weeks after he was born—my own doctor for a routine post-partum check-up. We did the usual: stirrups, paper robe, *How you feeling, Feeling okay.* She took some X-rays—"Normal procedure," she'd said, "Just checking things out." Then, she asked if we could talk in her office. I remember it was nondescript, sterile even—no art or personal photos, like she never spent time there. We sat on opposite sides of the desk. She had my X-rays spread out before her. She stared at them for a really, really long time.

Then she said, "Oh."

She told me that my ovary was the size of a cherry tomato. And a cell the size of a grain of rice had grown into a tumor the size of a tangerine.

When I look down the line of my life, there are all these moments—my parents splitting up, my first heartbreak, losing a job

I loved—and I cried or panicked or locked myself in a room playing Smiths albums on repeat, whatever; I *felt* something. But when that doctor told me I had a tumor? Nothing. I felt nothing. Not in that doctor's office. Not telling my husband later that night. Not walking into surgery the following week. *Nothing*—right up until I opened my eyes and my doctor said she'd got it; everything was fine. One day, you're already dead; the next day, you're back at the office. I cried and thanked her and drank my juice. After all of *that*, she said, "You're lucky you got pregnant. If it hadn't been for the ultrasound, we might not have caught it in time."

In that moment, I knew exactly what I felt.

Something.

It was so close. Like when I'm on my dad's fishing boat in the Pacific, out there in the middle of nowhere, surrounded by blue, and can't tell when the sky begins and the water ends. It is vast. It is still. It is—

Something.

Or: for years, I lived in Humboldt Park, west at North and Kimball, and a few blocks from my apartment was this church. It was really small, not more than a storefront, but the singing that came out of that place was like nothing I'd ever heard. Every Sunday I'd get coffee at Dunkin Donuts and sit on the curb outside that church. I never went in—there are a lot of things that happen inside of a church that I know are not for me—but sitting outside? I could have the parts that felt like—

Something.

Or: my son is three years old now. He is awesome. He thinks he's Superman, which sounds very cute, except we live on the third floor and he keeps trying to fly. Last week he stood at our balcony door in his red and blue costume, nose pressed to the glass, and said, "Mommy, let me out. I'll put my arms out far; I'll go high up in the sky." And of course, what I did then was check that lock, but what I realized is this: our children save us. They illuminate what's been there all along. They make us better than we ever thought we could be. My son really is Superman. Without him, I'd have never had an ultrasound. Without him, the tangerine could have grown into a grapefruit. Without him, I might not be sitting here today, and for that, I will believe. Call it God, if you like. Call it The Divine. Call it Not Atheist.

I call it a start.

A THIRD OF YOUR LIFE

PEOPLE THROW THE WORD "CRAZY" AROUND A LOT—*those kids are crazy! What are you, crazy? I'm going crazy!*—but I know what crazy really means because of this guy Eddie. He lives above the breakfast place where I work, and every day he comes downstairs to eat. He's a big dude with a shaved head, moustache, and he only wears cut-off jean shorts and knee-high suede moccasins with fringe; that's all, so you can really see his whole nine yards: hairy back, flabby front. And he sweats a lot—appetizing? Not so much. My boss, Josh, gave him the whole *no shoes no shirt no service* song and dance, so Eddie went out and got a suede fringed vest that matched the moccasins. I figure he must freeze in the winter and now, one of those awful Chicago Julys, he's *got* to be dying under all that animal skin. But it isn't my place to ask. What I can ask is, "You want some coffee, Eddie?"

"Absolutely not," he always says. "I don't condone that sort of behavior." Then he goes on to explain what caffeine can do if you mix it with other chemicals—Lithium or Prozac or Wellbutrin or Lexapro or Celexa, 'cause those are the ones he's on.

"Okay, then," I say, and get him juice instead, followed by a red pepper benedict, the Garden section of the Trib, and two crossword puzzles. After that he gets up, lays down a twenty, and goes to work at the Sealy Posturepedic warehouse, driving pillows around in a great big truck.

"How's your mattress, Megan?" he asks me, very seriously.

"It's fine," I say, 'cause what else do you say?

"Gotta be," he says. "You spend a third of your life on your mattress."

I don't know if he realizes that we've had this same conversation, right down to the sentence structure, for nearly a year; that because of him I can define such terms as *Depressive Pseudodementia* and *Psychomotor Retardation* with medical exactitude. It's actually helpful, this front row seat to crazy, 'cause lately I've been thinking I might be going crazy myself.

Every morning, I get to the restaurant at 6 a.m. I walk from table to table, putting napkins down at every right corner. Then I take the same walk, putting spoons on the right side of every napkin. Then, around again with knives, and then—*then*—the forks. *Napkin, spoon, knife, fork; napkin, spoon, knife, fork*; and I've been working here for, what, five years now? I never was very good at math, but that's a lot of forks, right? *Right?* So what would happen if I switched it up a bit? Maybe go napkin, *fork*, knife, spoon; or knife, *then* fork; or maybe really let loose and put the forks on the *right* side of the napkin. Would the world start spinning backwards? Would the glaciers melt, meteors crash, or humanity find some common ground?—who knows! *Not me!* So last week, on Monday, I put down all forks. No knives or spoons, just three forks on every napkin. Then, on Tuesday, I didn't put down any forks at all, just all knives and spoons; on Wednesday, no spoons. So, maybe you're thinking *This isn't very interesting, Megan, I've got better things to think about than cutlery*—and I get it, I do—but it's important that you stick with me here 'cause this is how I lost my mind. For real. Not *Oh I'm going crazy*, like we say eight hundred times a day, but serious. *Certifiable.*

"Uhm, Megan?" Molly asked after a few days of resetting the silverware I'd just set. She'd never dream of second-guessing me—she's only been working here a couple months, and I've been here five years; five years, waiting tables at the same exact place—*five.* "What are you doing?"

"I don't know, Molly," I said. I turned around and faced her, her curly hair and careful smile and fistfuls of forks. "Maybe I'm going crazy."

She laughed. "Totally," she said. "That happens to me all the time."

I pointed a fork at her and said, "I'm serious. I might be seriously crazy."

"You're seriously crazy," Andy said, when I suggested we go dancing. We'd just picked up some takeout from Penny's Noodles and were driving back to his place.

"Let's go!" I said again, having that fun little fantasy where you've got a rose between your teeth and your boyfriend's in tight black pants with a magical, wonderful ass, dipping you low and dragging you slowly up his torso. "I saw a sign back there, let's try it!"

He stopped at a red light and turned to face me. "I'm from

Marquette Park," he said, as if the South Side was where this question would die. "Besides," he went on, "it's almost time for CSI."

This is what we do, me and Andy. We get take-out food and go home at the end of a long day, mine at the restaurant and his at the ad firm. We snuggle up on the couch and drink beers and relax. He'll have one arm around me, and sometimes we'll make out. And if that gets heavy, we'll go into the bedroom for sex, after which he falls asleep fast 'cause he works all these hours. And that's when I lay there, listening to him breathe. It's something between breathing and snoring, actually, with a little bit of spit rolling in the back of his throat. Sometimes he whistles through his nose. I listen to this every night.

Every night.

Every night.

Every night, and then the alarm goes off at five, and I'm at work by six, setting up the restaurant: *napkin, spoon, knife, fork,* creamers in the bowls. "What kind of toast would you like with that, sir?" In my hands are the coffee cups, and I imagine throwing them, or flinging plates like Frisbees; they'd smash against the wall right above the line of customers' heads, and it would be so, so, so satisfying. But instead I say, "Would you like hash browns or side salad?" to the three-top at table seven and "Citrus vinaigrette or lemon tarragon?" to the lady on nineteen. And to Eddie, I say, "You want some coffee?"

"I don't condone such behavior," he says, and this is our routine—red pepper benedicts, crossword puzzles, *a third of your life on a mattress.* And on we go, every day, Monday through Friday. Eddie never comes in on the weekends. On the weekends, it's not breakfast, but *brunch.* Brunch in Chicago is an almost religious experience. The restaurant is packed, people wait over an hour for a table—it's way too much for Eddie to handle.

The day it happened was a Sunday, one of those awful 90 degree mornings where the humidity wraps over you like a blanket. All the customers waited inside for their tables, to be near the A/C, and me and Molly and the other girls could barely shove through the bodies. "Excuse me!" we said, carrying plates high over our heads. "Coming though! Look out, this stains!" I was behind the counter pouring mimosas when Eddie came in, all bare, hairy chest and dangly fringe. He looked shocked to see so many people here, in *his* place, interrupting *his* breakfast, his routine. I saw him talk to Josh by the front door. I couldn't hear them over all the people, but I figured Josh told him he'd have to wait.

That wouldn't go over very well.

Eddie stood for a minute, oblivious to the stares he was getting 'cause of his clothes, then turned to the nearest customer— some dad with a comb-over and pleated pants. *Don't*, I thought, not knowing what he was doing but sure that he shouldn't as he grabbed the guy's arm and whispered something. The dad's eyes widened, and he backed up a couple steps into the lady behind him. A sort of domino-effect happened then—customers backing into busboys backing into waitresses, with Eddie moving forward through the mayhem, grabbing anyone who got in his way, whispering something to each of them. Eventually he made it to the counter—to me. His eyes were glazed, a thin layer of milk coating the iris, and I knew he wasn't seeing me as he wrapped one meaty fist around my elbow and tightened, his fingers pushing through my skin, hitting bone. And it hurt, it hurt, but I knew he wouldn't hear me if I said, "Let me go, Eddie," or "You want some coffee, Eddie?" or "Did you forget the Lexapro this morning, Eddie?" He wouldn't hear my words 'cause he didn't hear his own, like somebody else was speaking through his mouth as he whispered, "If you don't get out of here, I'll take you outside and smash your head on the sidewalk. I'll hold it between my palms and pound it into the concrete."

When I think back on this, I don't remember feeling scared. I remember feeling sad. He was so completely alone.

In the end, Josh called the cops and Eddie was 86'd—couldn't come into the restaurant without an automatic arrest. I'd see him sometimes, driving the big 'ol Sealy truck packed with pillows, and he'd always ask how my mattress was.

"Gotta be fine," he'd say. "You spend a third of your life on a mattress." I'd repeat those words at night—*a third of your life, a third of your life*—as I listened to Andy breathe the spit-sloggy in and outs, feeling my mattress below me, watching the ceiling above me, watching the clock: one o'clock, two o'clock, three. And by then, I was imagining all the things I could stick up Andy's nose: drinking straws, uncapped Sharpies, the corkscrew for wine.

And one night, a month or so after Eddie went crazy, I got out of bed and went to the kitchen. I opened the silverware drawer and took out the knives and forks and spoons, and then I opened the oven and stuck them all in. There was still a lot of space in there, so I got the dishes and put them in, too; and the pots and pans, and the blender, and the electric juicer; and everything on the spice rack. By then, there was too much stuff in the oven, so I took it all out and tried to put it back in a rational manner, like when you're packing for some big trip. You roll up the underwear and the socks and stuff them in your running shoes. You put the extra batteries in with your toiletries. You fold your flip flops into your sweaters—you make it fit. I would make it fit. *Fit*, goddammit! And suddenly, the overhead light came on, and there was Andy, standing over me.

I've since tried to imagine what he saw that night—the girl he thought he knew so well, squatting on the tiled kitchen floor with her blue nightgown hiked up around her thighs, surrounded by foodstuffs and spices and flatware and Tupperware. My eyes must have been glassy as I looked up at him, my hair wild.

He was very still as he sized me up. Then he asked, "What's going on in here?" as though I might have a logical explanation.

"Your nose whistles," I said.

He just stood there, not making any sudden movements.

"Every night," I went on. "Every night it whistles, every night I listen, and I figured I should get up this time and do something different so that every night wouldn't be the same night as last night—"

That's when the alarm starts buzzing in our bedroom, and it's time to go to work. *Napkin, spoon, fork, knife.* Creamers in the bowls. Coffee decaf regular. And at nine-thirty, we open and the place fills up. It doesn't matter where my mind is—my body knows what to do. It's muscle memory that makes your latte, classical conditioning that reaches for the juice; like, how someone can ask *What's up?* and you say *Fine,* 'cause you assume they've said, *How are you?*

I know what to do and I do it—it's routine—except today is different. Today, Molly says, "Hey, look," and points out the front windows of the restaurant. It's one of those warm, perfect Chicago September mornings. Every customer waiting for a table is standing around *outside*: moms and dads, girlfriends and boyfriends, tables of six or seven friends meeting for brunch, all of them on the sidewalk looking at the sky with their arms in the air and their hands held palms up to catch the snow. Snow—it's snowing, white fluffy flakes falling mid-September. But when I get closer to the windows and out the front door, I can see what it really is: feathers. Hundreds of feathers floating in the air, and I stand on the sidewalk and tilt my head back. There, leaning out his window above us with an army knife and a pillow, is Eddie in all his fringe. He splits the pillow open with the knife, holds two opposite corners, and shakes it 'til the feathers fly. Then he reaches behind him and grabs another pillow, pillow after pillow. "How's your mattress, Megan?" he yells down from the window, and I close my eyes and let the feathers brush my face.

It feels really wonderful.

Even if it is kind of crazy.

THOSE WHO WERE THERE

WHEN I WAS EIGHTEEN, I accidentally went to bed with a guy who had a glass testicle. I say accidentally because I'd been trying to go to bed with someone else, someone with what I can only assume were normal testicles. But in the end that didn't pan out, and the guy with the glass testicle was, you know—*there*.

I remember feeling anxious about the testicle because earlier that year I'd sliced my hand open, which I'd like to say happened because I was out living life in some young and fabulous way, but the truth is that I wanted to see what the snow looked like inside of a snow globe—laundry detergent, in case you're wondering; the kind with the flakes—a discovery which was decidedly not worth seven stitches across the center of my palm, tiny and meticulous and bloody beneath the florescent lights of the ER. And that, my friends, is what I was imagining as the guy with the glass testicle slid around on top of me: one false move and back to the ER, except this time, it wouldn't be my hand; it would be my *insides*.

The fact that I thought his testicle would be inside of me is a perfect illustration of my eighteen-year-old understanding of sex. In my defense, I'd only been with one other guy, my sort-of, sometimes high school boyfriend, Jimmy, and our furtive fumblings in the prop room after play practice were more *is it in there/is it not* than they were actual sex, which was beside the point because, so far as I was concerned, we were in love. Like, epically. If Sid and Nancy, Patti and Robert, F. Scott and Zelda had been lame, sheltered, adolescent Midwesterners, we'd be them. So you can imagine my heartbreak when we broke up senior year due to future plans. Mine of which included college in Boston, and his of which included fucking Shelby Lapinski. She would be, you know, *there*.

"You have to get over that guy," my new friend Jill would tell me. "You should have sex with Ira Birnham." Ira Birnham lived in our dorm. His parents owned a place on an island called Martha's Vineyard where Bill Clinton had a summer home, and sometimes, when I passed Ira in the hall on the way to the cafeteria, I thought I smelled the ocean. *Maybe I should have sex with him*, I thought, but then I went back to Michigan for Christmas break, and Jimmy was in my driveway in a used RV. "Here's my plan," he said, after a very fast *I'm sorry, Shelby's a bitch, can't live without you, is it in there/is it not*. "This summer, I'll pick you up in Boston, and we'll travel around the country. The RV doesn't, like, drive right now, but I'll get it fixed and then—the story of our life will begin."

The fact that I thought this could actually happen is a perfect illustration of my eighteen-year-old understanding of reality.

The day Jimmy was supposed to pick me up was the same day we moved out of the dorm. I had just finished packing my stuff, Jill had just sat down to roll a joint, and Ira Birnham had just stopped in to say that we should look him up if we ever came to the vineyard. "I told you to have sex with him," Jill had just said, and that's when the phone rang.

"I don't know what happened!" Jimmy said into my ear. "One second I'm driving, the next second I smell smoke, the next second my back end's up in flames. And I'm lucky I got out when I did 'cause like a minute later they caught the gas tank."

"What caught the gas tank?" I said.

"The flames," he said.

"So the RV—" I started, and he finished—"Exploded."

Think about how hard it is to get over your first love. Part of me wonders, if it had been any other reason—he didn't want to travel, he was out of money, he was back with Shelby—anything else, maybe I'd have forgiven him. Maybe I'd still be obsessed with him, still waiting for the story of our lives to begin. But that day, that glorious day, Jesus Christ our Lord gave me a sign from the Heavens. It said: MEGAN. WALK AWAY. AND TO BE SURE THERE IS NO CONFUSION ON THIS ISSUE, I'M GOING TO SET FIRE TO HIS RV, WHICH I HOPE YOU UNDERSTAND IS A METAPHOR.

I understand, Jesus, I whispered. *A metaphor.*

"... so I'm stuck outside of Battle Creek," Jimmy was saying, unaware of my religious experience. "I called a tow truck, but I need you to—"

I hung up.

Almost immediately, the phone started ringing again.

I looked at it. Then I looked at Jill and said, "I don't know what to do." I had nowhere to live until school started in the fall;

no job, no internship, eighteen and stupid, certainly. But also, for the first time in my life—free.

"I have a plan," she said, handing me the joint. The phone kept ringing while we smoked, and it kept ringing as we loaded my stuff into Jill's car. Sometimes, if I listen really hard, I can still hear it.

Jill's plan went like this:

1) Get off the ferry on Martha's Vineyard.

2) Find Ira Birnham. Exactly how we'd accomplish this wasn't clear. She kept saying, "He told us to look him up," but this was 1993, pre-cell phone, pre-everyone on the internet all the goddamn time, and do you know how many Birnham's are in the phone book? Anyhow, she was sure we'd find him, at which point—

3) I would have sex with him, and—

4) We'd stay for the summer at his parents' fancy beach house, which to her, seemed completely plausible.

This is what actually happened:

1) Jill met some people on the ferry who said we could stay at their place so long as she shared her mushrooms.

2) I was like, "Mushrooms, the food?"

3) She was like, "No."

4) You guys, mushrooms are awesome! Colors are like, bright; you can't tell where the sky ends and the ocean begins; and everyone you meet is a part of your family. On the way to wherever my new family was taking me, we stopped by the beach to pick up their friend Steve, which is such an amazing word to feel inside your mouth! Let's all say it together—

STEVE.

—and when I first saw him, he was upside down in some totally cosmic yoga headstand with the sun setting orange and purple behind him. I was like GAAAAAAH, and Jill was like, "You should have sex with him."

"Aren't I supposed to have sex with Ira Birnham?" I asked.

She was like, "I don't care who you have sex with, just have sex with someone, anyone, everyone as soon as possible," which at the time was so fucking profound, so I ran towards the sunset, put my head in the sand next to upside-down Steve, and said, "We can have sex if you want."

If you're ever in need of a pick-up line, that one totally works.

My new family and new boyfriend, Steve, lived in the woods—about ten-or-so twenty-something kids squatting in tents around a makeshift fire-pit. They washed their clothes in the ocean and hung them on tree branches. They grew their own weed and slept under the stars. To me, mid-mushrooms and stupid with 19th Century romance novels, this was the most perfect living situation in the history of ever, and I decided to stay there for the rest of my life, eating green peppers roasted like Marshmallows and having sex with Steve in his tiny, two-person tent, bending our bodies into totally awkward positions to get out of our clothes in that tiny, cramped space. I remember he tasted like salt water from showering in the ocean. I remember thinking now the story of my life will begin. I remember him looking deep into my eyes, almost climbing down inside my brain, and saying, "Before this goes any further, I have to tell you something."

In the twenty years that have passed since then, there has been some version of this moment every time I've had sex. "I have something to tell you," they say, and then: I have a girlfriend and/or boyfriend; I'm leaving tomorrow for LA and/or Morocco; I have crabs and/or herpes and/or Gonorrhea; and my personal favorite: I have a phobia of naked feet, so can you please put your socks back on. In all of those situations, I have known what to say or at the very least, faked it well, but riddle me this: what do you say when he looks deep in your eyes and says, "I have a glass testicle"?

Later, in the thick of it, I'd worry that the glass might cut me.

Later still, long after I'd left the vineyard, I'd wonder how he lost the testicle in the first place. Birth defect? Disease? Seesaw accident?

Still later, while looking at testicular prosthesis on the internet,[1] I'd learn that glass hasn't been used since the 1940s. Why, for the love of God, would he lie? About *that*?

And later—still, still later—while working on this essay, I'd realize: of all the people I've slept with because they were, you know, *there*, he is the only one I really remember.

But of course, in the moment, in that tent, drugged and naked and stupid and free, I didn't say any of that.

I said what I think any of us would have:

"Dude. Can I touch it?"

It felt sort of like a snow globe.

Footnote:

1. I should not have to explain the American phenomenon of Looking At Stupid Shit on the Internet, but here's what happened: In 2005, my then-boyfriend/now-husband and I adopted a super-mutt puppy named Mojo, and of course we got him fixed because there are already enough adorable puppies out there needing homes (in fact, why don't you adopt one or two or five right now!).

So one night, we're sitting on the couch with Mojo asleep between us, lying on his back with his little paws in the air, and Christopher looks down at him and says, "Do you think he knows we took away his testicles?" I don't answer this question, hoping that if I ignore a conversation about testicles it will go away, but Christopher has had a drink or two or five, so he grabs the nearest laptop (re: mine) and plugs TESTICLES FOR PETS into Google, which brings him to a site called Neuticles. And *of course*, we have to do shots and read aloud from the testimonials.

"I've put off neutering Crooked Joe for months, and when I found out about Neuticles and spoke to them, it made me feel better about neutering. Joe not only looks the same now—but doesn't know he's missing anything."

"Frodo never knew he lost anything and is just a happier little dog since he's been neutered with Neuticles."

"Neuticles were the absolute least I could do."

At one point, Christopher got up to make popcorn, and I went to check my email or something. Since I'd just been looking at testicular prosthesis, every ad on the entire Internet now thought I was in the market. Still to this day, they think I'm in the market, and since they want me to be as informed as possible, they send me all sorts of products and info sites including history sites—hence how I found out about the glass. The end.

HOW TO SAY THE RIGHT THING WHEN THERE'S NO RIGHT THING TO SAY

for T.

YOUR FRIEND IS GOING THROUGH SOMETHING HARD, and you don't know what to say. There are words and there are words and there are words.

Stop saying them. Stop trying.

Instead, pick her up in your Jeep. Don't worry if you don't have one. This is your imagination; you get to have cool stuff. You get to drive a Jeep and wear Marc Jacobs and super cool aviator sunglasses, even though you don't usually wear sunglasses because you sunburn easily (one time in college, you got a bitch of a sunburn *around your sunglasses*, which left weird raccoon circles on your face for months, so now you just squint). Your friend, Sheila—we'll call her Sheila—has on a black vinyl catsuit—think Trinity—and one of those Marilyn Monroe scarves around her head so that her shiny, perfect hair doesn't get mussed in the wind—because, of course, the top is down, and you're driving super-fast, like Action Movie Chase Scene fast, so fast you left your infant son at home because, even in your imagination, it's irresponsible to drive that fast with a kid in the car, which is why in real life you have one of those BABY ON BOARD signs suction-cupped to the back window of your Honda, because drivers in Chicago have a lot of road rage—yes they do—and you don't want anybody fucking around when your kid's in the car. So you hung that sign because that'll make them drive nice, right?

You and Sheila hang your hands out the zipped-down windows, your palms pushing against the wind, and in your other hand you have an extra-large, extra-caffeinated Frappuccino with bourbon because yum. But this means you don't have any hands on the wheel, so, okay then, it's a magic Jeep, and you can drive it with your mind. Or maybe the Jeep can talk! Like Kitt, from *Knight Rider*! Maybe the Jeep is Kitt from *Knight Rider*, except a Jeep instead of a Trans Am, and you can talk to it or think at it, thus keeping your hands free for the wind against your fingers and caffeinated alcoholic beverages, which in real life you're not currently drinking because you're breastfeeding, but ZOMFG you would so totally kill for a Maker's Mark right now.

So anyhow, you're driving these precarious winding trails through the mountains, passing ginormous valleys and snow-capped peaks. After a while, the road starts running parallel to a train because, in your mind, all trains are on windy tracks through the mountains, like duh. You briefly consider hijacking it—getting the Jeep right alongside and then jumping onboard with some of that *Crouching Tiger, Hidden Dragon* shit, saving whoever's being held against their will or stealing back the medicine that someone very corrupt stole from dying villagers because wouldn't that be awesome?—but then, you look at Sheila, your beautiful friend who is right now trying to slay a dragon so huge and deadly it could engulf a whole city with a single exhale.

Sheila doesn't need to hijack a train right now.

What she needs is a friend.

"Go faster," you say to Kitt the Jeep.

"Faster."

"Go faster than this train."

The tires are screeching now, burning into the asphalt. Sheila's scarf comes loose and whips away, but it's okay because you own Neiman Marcus and you'll get her another tomorrow. Right now you're chasing the train, passing the train, ahead of the train, *way* ahead of the train, far enough ahead to pull over, grab Sheila by the hand, run to the side of the tracks, and—

Wait.

You'll feel it coming first, the ground trembling beneath your shoes.

Next, you'll hear it: the whistle, the wheels churning on the tracks.

Then, it's there: the enormous front engine, car after car behind it for miles, curling behind the winding track. It's coming closer, faster, getting louder, *louder*, LOUDER. YOU CAN'T HEAR ANYTHING OVER THE IMMENSITY OF SOUND. You're so close to the tracks, your toes a few feet from the hammered metal, and when it passes you, you scream.

At first, Sheila looks at you like you're crazy which, frankly, isn't anything new. She's been looking at you that way since you were both kids in OshKosh B'Gosh in the mud in Southeast Michigan. Then in college, shaking her head in disgust as you poured Everclear into the Kool-Aid. And now, screaming your head off over the relentless roar of a passing train. And okay, fine, whatever, maybe you are crazy, but sometimes crazy is the only way to get through.

Sheila shuts her eyes, then opens her mouth, and now she's screaming, too—both of you screaming holy hell as the train pounds past, car after car. And you scream and you scream 'cause there's so much inside that needs to get out—anger and longing and no sleep and time moving too fast and sorrow and fear. You scream so long, so loud, it's like your throats are bleeding, rubbed raw on the inside. And by the time the last car passes, it's all been drained, like you're sponges squeezed dry. You sit on the ground, exhausted by the energy it takes to let go, and lay backwards in the grass. The sun shines on your faces. The backs of your eyelids glow red. There's a breeze, and the grass is soft, and you move your arms and legs to make snow angels even though there's no snow. It feels nice to be so deliciously empty, so open for new things, like spring and laughter and the future and new memories and newly remembered experiences and all the things you've been lucky enough to do, and the knowledge that you still have, at the very least, this single, perfect day to live.

After a long time, you get up. You hold out your hand to help Sheila to her feet—she is, after all, wearing a catsuit, and that shit's hard to navigate. Her face is dripping mascara from crying, but underneath that, she's smiling.

It's wonderful to see her smile.

It's the most wonderful thing in the universe.

You go back to the Jeep, except it's not a jeep anymore; it's something more practical, but still edgy. Maybe an Element? or a RAV4? In the backseat, your infant son is strapped in his car seat, laughing in his sleep. You and Sheila change into comfy clothes because couture and catsuits are, sadly, not for R&R, and you drive back down the mountain, still with your arms out the windows, but now the wind pushes the backs of your hands instead of the palms. After a while, you pass a little cafe with outdoor seating. You order wine. You watch the sun set over those snowcapped peaks, color exploding over the sky: yellow to red to midnight blue. That's when you tell her how sorry you are, how your thoughts are with her and her family. You tell her it sucks, sucks, sucks, and nothing is fair and that sucks. You say words like *strength* and *time*, even though you know how many others have told her those same words, told her anything and everything in the hope it's the right thing to say.

But it's not.

There isn't any right thing to say.

So you just stop talking. You hand her your son. He wraps his tiny fists around her thumbs, and the three of you watch the stars. Out here, they're for real, not like in the city where you can only see one or two but thousands, millions, millions of millions, and they're all so goddamn beautiful.

I BOP

I'M NINE YEARS OLD, my jeans are pegged so tightly at the ankles that I can't feel my feet, and a single ponytail—well ratted with Aquanet and a pick comb—juts out over my ear like a handle to my head. I have a pink plastic boom box, a cassette tape of Cyndi Lauper's *She's So Unusual*, and I'm standing in front of the bathroom mirror, dancing side-to-side and singing "She Bop" into a whisk.

This was before Tipper Gore's Parents Music Resource Center and the Filthy Fifteen—a list of songs with questionable content including Prince, AC/DC, and "She Bop," because apparently it taught adolescent girls how to masturbate and I'm like, Tipper, let's get real, okay? I did not learn how to masturbate from Cyndi Lauper. I learned to masturbate from a female stagehand in a community player's production of *Charlie and the Chocolate Factory*. I was playing Violet Beauregard's mother, minding my own business while my daughter turned into a blueberry night after night, while over at the University of Michigan, that stagehand was getting liberated in some Womyn-with-a-Y Studies class and on closing night, she gave me book called *Sex For One*. To educate me. To guide me. To help me get in touch with my inner Venus, which I most certainly did not want to do. What I wanted to do was stand in front of the bathroom mirror and sing along with Cyndi.

"She bop—he bop—a—we bop, I bop—you bop—a—they bop, Be bop—be bop—a—lu—bop, I hope he will understand, She bop—"

"She *what?*" my mother asked. She was in the next room, grading fourth grade spelling tests.

"Bop," I told her, squinting at my reflection just like Cyndi did in the "Time After Time" video. "She bop."

"She *can't* bop," my mother said. "Bop is not a verb."

Grammar was an important thing in our family. While my friend Becky and I were welcome to ride our bikes to the library, *me* and Becky most certainly could not.

"It is so a verb," I said, irritated that my performance had been interrupted. I put down the whisk, hit stop on my boom box, and stood in the doorway so she could see my indignation. "Bop is *totally* an action word."

My mother looked at me over her glasses. "Try it out in a sentence—" I always had to try stuff out in sentences— "We bop, I bop, they bop," she demonstrated, oblivious that she was reciting lyrics. "You bop, he bop—"

"See, that's grammar!" I said.

"It is not grammar," she said.

And I said, "Cyndi *Lauper* says it's grammar!"

I'd recently watched that episode of the Cosby show where Vanessa wants to wear makeup and her mother says no. Vanessa's thirteen and snotty and says, "Rebecca's mother lets her wear makeup!" And Claire says, "I am not Rebecca's mother! If you want to live by her rules, go live in her house. But under my roof, you will do as I say!" I think I imagined a similar exchange between me and my own mother—I mean, my mother *and I*—but it didn't happen. She wasn't some sitcom character with scripted dialogue; she was a very real woman trying to juggle a marriage and a career and a kid. And sometimes I made her crazy, and sometimes worried, and often, proud. But the thing with Cyndi Lauper and the grammar? That just made her tired. I remember she took off her glasses and looked up at the ceiling as though the rules of parenting might be stenciled in the paint. "Someday," she said, "if you decide to have children of your own, you'll understand."

Memory is a tricky thing. I can generally remember the scene, and usually, the tenor of voices and general subject matter—but exact dialogue is a rarity. Not in this scenario. "If you decide to have children of your own," she said, "you'll understand." I remember it so clearly, every word. "If you decide," she said. "If you decide."

Every month or so, I come across an article telling me what a woman or a girl should or should not do. How she should and should not act. What she can and cannot say. Can she have a job *and* a family? Can she have a family and go to college? Can she go to college, period? Can she be a rock singer or a CEO or a writer? Can she write if she has a child? If she has a second child? When are you going to have your second child? When are you going to get married? When are you going to get a 401K? Did you bake the baked goods for the bake sale or *buy* the baked goods for the bake sale? Did you stop calling yourself a feminist because Susan Sarandon stopped calling herself a feminist? Did you opt in or opt out, nevermind any mention of the financial position a woman would need to be in to make that choice in the first damn place and please, please please please, can we stop? Can we find a way to tell our stories, weigh our options, get advice and/or back-up and/or support when and if we need it without being told, every month, what we should or should not do, can or cannot say?

If you decide, my mom said to me when I was nine. She said it when I was fifteen, too. And twenty-six. And thirty-three. And yesterday.

If you decide.

In the moment, of course, I missed all of this nuance. All I heard was *Someday You'll Understand.* When you're nine, nothing is as infuriating as being told you can't understand something until later. I flounced back into the bathroom, turned the pink boom box up as loud as it would go, and faced my reflection: the ridiculous ponytail, an off-the-shoulder sweatshirt a la *Flashdance. Never*, I told myself. *Never, ever, ever are you going to grow up and get stupid about important things the way grown-ups sometimes are.*

82 DEGREES

IT WAS TWENTY BELOW, one of those horrible Chicago winter nights with a blizzard advisory, and even with three layers of gortex, your fingers are still ice in your mittens and every breath freezes your insides. If you're smart, you stay home, wrapped under afghans with hot chocolate and thermal socks—but me? I was out there, midnight on a Wednesday, trying to dig my car from its parking spot, which was totally futile 'cause every shovelful of snow was immediately replaced with more snow. An easy eight inches on the ground already, and did I mention I was wearing heels? And a dress? And two coats of mascara, frozen in black icicles. My entire everything was like ten seconds away from hypothermia, and right about now you're thinking, "Were you insane? Why were you out there?"

Because of a guy.

"Who is *that?*" said Ellie, one of the waitresses I worked with. It was a particularly slow morning, and the entire staff was packed behind the coffee bar, watching Christopher eat pancakes on the other side of the restaurant.

"He's *cute!*" said Sharon.

"He's *tall!*" said Beth.

"He visits Megan all the time," said Molly. "*And—*" They leaned forward. "—he tips 25%."

"Ohhhhhhh," they all said, because 25% is totally hot.

"Come on," I said. "We're just friends."

They laughed.

"No, really," I said. "We're not dating."

"How come?" they asked. "Is he weird/is he an addict/is he gay?" These were characteristics of my previous boyfriends. Christopher was none of those things. He was smart, and funny, and one time, I'd had a few too many, and he gave me a piggy-back ride from his car to my front door. Then he set me down and I looked up at him—he's six-five, so you've really got to bend your neck—and I know this'll sound crazy, but it was like a giant YOU ARE HERE sign hung above us, as though my whole life had been leading up to this. single. moment.

"It's worse than weird," I told the waitresses. "He has a girl-friend."

Beckie.

With an ie.

And let me tell you, this girl? She was... I mean, I can't even... I met her one time, at a dinner party, and she was...

Fine.

Perfectly nice and pretty and *fine.*

It would've been easier if she'd been horrible, if I had a reason to hate her beside the fact that she had him and I didn't, but—nothing. Christopher and I were friends. We went to the movies—friends. We met up for drinks—friends. We read each other's writing—still friends! And for nearly a year I ignored the fact that I was so in love with him I could barely breathe.

Right up until that frozen, twenty-below night.

I was in my apartment with the heat blasting, buried under the covers with Kafka's collected short stories. That summer, I'd be moving to Prague for a year to teach a study abroad program, and I was working my way through all Kafka's novels, diaries, biographies—FYI: if you're going to read as much Kafka as I was reading, please have plenty of Prozac on hand 'cause that shit can mess with your psyche. I must have jumped ten feet when the phone rang.

"Hello? What? Hi!"

It was Christopher, asking me to meet him for a drink.

"Now?" I said. "It's nearly midnight, and like a million below zero. Have you seen outside? My window is a solid sheet of white, and you know I hate snow—"

"Beckie and I broke up," he said.

I LOVE SNOW! IT'S FLUFFY! YOU CAN MAKE ICE CREAM OUT OF IT, JUST ADD MILK AND SUGAR AND—

"Meet you in a half hour?" he said.

And I knew my entire life was about to change.

I'd like to talk, just for moment, about the act of Getting Ready. Christopher and I met for drinks all the time, and usually I'd run out the door in jeans and sneakers, but this was different. This wasn't just going out to meet Christopher. It was GOING OUT TO MEET CHRISTOPHER. It required an OUTFIT. A HAIR STYLE. EVENING MAKEUP, which is significantly more time-consuming than day makeup, but nevertheless an absolute necessity because this was the night I convinced my future husband that he couldn't live without me.

Hence the high heels in eight inches of snow.

We met at Ezuli, this late night place on Milwaukee Avenue. It's not around anymore, but you've been somewhere like it: dark, candles on every table, a glow coming off the bar where backlights caught the colored bottles. The place was dead when I got there, and I positioned myself at the bar, trying to find my most attractive angle: face left, face right; legs crossed, not crossed; do I lean forward on my elbows, looking contemplative or sit straight, back arched, chest out, stomach sucked in, *look thin, look thin, don't breath, look thin—*

"Are you okay?" Christopher asked, appearing suddenly behind me and peeling out of his coat, hat, gloves, scarf, and sweater. He looked great. It was the first time I'd ever seen him single.

"What? Hi! Yes?—wait, what was the question?"

"Are you okay?" he repeated. "You're twitching."

We ordered hot, steaming whiskey and settled in for The Talk; you know, the one where he tells me—his friend—all about the break up, and at opportune times I say to him—my friend— "Oh my god," or "No way!" or "I know," except I was having a really hard time listening to him because 1) The music was really loud, so we had to sort of lean into each other to talk, and 2) He smelled really great, like chocolate and amber and OMG *sex right now* and I'm sorry, but 3) It's really hard to be a good friend when all you want to do is climb someone like a tree.

Tell him, I thought. *Just tell him.*

"We were together for so long," he was saying, and I reached across the table for his hand. "I don't remember the last time I was single," he said.

I opened my mouth to say it: "Christopher—"

"I just need to be single," he said.

And I said, "I—wait. What?"

"I need to be single for a while," he repeated.

I pulled back my hands.

"I'm not going to date 'til it's 82 degrees," he said, and I looked out the front window: the screaming wind, the solid white wall of blizzard, the mountain of snow burying my car.

It was a really long winter.

Gray and frozen and stopping and starting a hundred times over, so one day, it's like *Sunshine! Chirping birds!* and the next, it's *Blizzard! Icy, dead things!* and all us poor Chicagoans can do is take it one day at a time. And complain, loudly, with very colorful language. But mostly, it's getting through the day, which for me, meant mornings at the brunch restaurant, afternoons teaching, and nights getting ready for Prague. *Who cares about men*, I'd think. *I'm going to Europe. I'll meet a Lord. With a ... manor. And enough money to buy my own damn summer, 'cause I'm over this cold, brittle darkness; this cabin-fever lockdown in my living room; this four separate layers before I leave the house.* But then!—I had That Day, that glorious day when you rush out the door in your four separate layers and immediately start sweating. The sun is high in the sky, you're blinded without sunglasses, and—*Oh my god! It's ... warm! There's like, grass! What's that?—a bird!* You go back inside, dropping fleece at the door, and get a stool to go to that top shelf in your closet with the shorts and the sandals. And of course, you haven't shaved your legs, and you're horribly pasty white, like you've been rolled in flour, but who cares!

You're saved! You're rescued from the tower, a steak in front of a starving populace. And what do you do on such an amazing day, Chicago?

You go to brunch!

The restaurant was packed, people waiting three hours or more for a table. They lined the sidewalk, baking in the brandnew sunshine, and crowded inside to get at the bar; sorbet mimosas, Peppar bloody marys, iced lattes with Kahlua—I couldn't keep up.

"Okay, okay, okay!" I yelled, lining glassware down the bar and pouring champagne from bottles in both hands. "I'm going as fast as I can!" That's when I looked up and saw Christopher.

Just his head at first, high above the rest of the crowd. But he shoved closer to the bar, closer to me. It had been a while since I'd seen him, steadily saying no to his invitations to drinks or movies. I'd told myself it was because I was leaving the country, but the truth was: I couldn't keep doing it. That YOU ARE HERE sign hanging above him hadn't gone away, and seeing him was salt on the wound.

It was easier when he had a girlfriend.

A girlfriend I could at least kill.

(in my mind).

(repeatedly).

"Hey," he said, once he got to the bar. "It's good to see you."

"Can I get you something to drink?" I said—'cause that's what I would say to a friend.

He paused—to this day I don't know what he was thinking—and then shook his head. "I'm waiting outside for a table," he said. And he turned and walked away.

"Are you crazy?" said Ellie, appearing at my elbow.

"He came here for you!" said Sharon, at my other elbow.

"And he's so cute!" said Beth.

"And tall!" said Molly.

I slammed the champagne bottles down on the bar. "Don't you all have tables?" I said, storming off towards the dish station for more glassware. The racks were empty and the washer steamed, meaning it needed a couple minutes to finish the cycle, so all I could do was stand there, listening to the bodies packing the bar, imagining the pile of drink orders growing, staring at the window in front of my face.

On that window was a thermometer, one of those outdoor digital jobs with the suction cup. It was 82 degrees.

Before, when I was single, I'd ask my friends in relationships how they knew. "What was it?" I'd say, wanting to hear some mathematical equation, some John Hughes character arc, some self-help step-by-step of finding my perfect person. If there were steps, I could execute them. I could work towards something. I could be an active participant in not only finding love but finding it now.

But it doesn't work that way. It works like this:

How do you know?

You just...do.

So what I did was walk out into the restaurant, pushing through the bodies to the door. Outside, the sun was blinding, the air warm against my too-white skin, and I looked up and down Milwaukee Avenue: everyone in their new summer clothes, waiting for pancakes, loving this new perfect day. And there, sitting on the sidewalk with a newspaper, was Christopher. I had no idea then that within the week, I'd move in with him. Within the month, he'd follow me to Prague. Within the year, we'd elope on Lake Michigan. And two years after that, our son would be born.

All I knew was in that moment, standing there in the 82 degrees?

I just...knew.

THE *OMG WE HAVE TO WRITE ABOUT THIS* LOOK

WHEN I FOUND OUT my story collection was being published, the first person I called was Jeff. He'd been there from the beginning: the writing and rewriting; submissions and rejections; and, most importantly, all of the living that inspired the stories in the first damn place.

We met up to celebrate. We drank champagne. "What did your editor say?" Jeff asked, and then added, gleefully, "You have an *editor!*" We giggled, drank more champagne, and talked about the stories. Jeff had been my first reader on all of them—except one.

"So," I said. We'd killed one bottle and ordered another. *Celebration!* "There's a story. In the book. It's about...us."

This is a tricky moment in the life of a writer. Let's call it... "The Talk." Historically, "The Talk" has referred to asking whomever you're dating whether or not they want to be exclusive, but for a writer, it's what happens when you've written about somebody close to you and you want their permission to publish it. It's a nerve-wracking thing. You squeezed your heart into this story! It's a great opportunity for your work! You changed the person's hair color and made them from Nova Scotia!—still, you care enough about the relationship to discuss it first.

For the record, I knew Jeff wouldn't care that I'd written about him. Not because I'd done it before (I had), and not because I'd disguised him enough that he'd never be recognized (I hadn't); rather, because he gets it. He, too, has done it. He, too, is a writer.

"Okay," he said, pouring more champagne. "Which part about us?"

"It was forever ago," I said. "We were living in Wicker Park, and we played that game called—"

He cut me off. "Oscar and Veronica?"

"Yes!"

"You wrote the Oscar and Veronica story?" There was something nervous about his voice, like how he sounded back when we were both interested in the same guy (this happened a lot); or when he told me that the guy I was dating was actually gay (this happened three times); or when he told me that he was gay (this happened once, fifteen years ago, back when I was hopelessly in love with him).

"Is there a problem with the Oscar and Veronica story?" I asked. "You know I've written way more personal things about you, like the time—"

He cut me off. "It's just weird, that's all."

"What?"

"I wrote the Oscar and Veronica story, too."

Here's how it worked: If Jeff called me Veronica, or I called him Oscar, it meant there was a cute guy within earshot, so we had to pretend to be brother and sister. The act was to appear natural, but be loud enough for the cute guy to overhear.

"Did mom call you?"

"Dad called last night."

"Remember when we were six and our cousin Johnny ate that lightbulb?"

It was silly and ridiculous and an absolute necessity because wherever Jeff and I went, everyone assumed we were together, thus contributing to all sorts of awkward situations and complicated emotions—the stuff that makes good stories.

To hear Jeff tell it, some ten-plus years ago we made a pact that each of us would, someday, write the Oscar and Veronica story. I don't remember that conversation, but I'm sure it could've happened that way; Jeff and I have made pacts to write a thousand different things: the time he brought me, as his date, to chaperone Howard Brown's gay prom; the time his very fabulous roommate used a loaf of French bread to teach me proper blow job technique; the time I told off his ex-boyfriend at a hot-dog stand; and on and on. The thing is, over all these years, all these stories, all these seemingly secret moments when we'd give each other the *OMG we have GOT to write about this* look—up until now, we've never actually *done* it.

When I think of literary friendship, I think of the heavyweights—Hemingway and Fitzgerald, Tolkien and C.S. Lewis, Emerson and Thoreau—their relationships are full of inspiration, arguments, jealousy, letters, reading, and late-night talks about life and literature. Are Jeff and I like that? Sometimes. I hand him drafts of stories I'm sure are done, and then he asks a single fucking question that keeps me awake for weeks. He's the one who put

Gabriel Garcia Marquez in my hands, who to this day is my favorite writer. When his editor asked for yet another rewrite, we spent hours in front of my bookshelf, trying to figure out how exactly writers pulled off this whole writing thing.

Every week, we sit in restaurants around Chicago, drinking champagne or coffee, depending on the hour, and typing from opposite sides of the table. Sometimes we talk—I know Jeff's fictional characters I better than I know some of my real-life relatives—but, more often than not, we work. We type. We *Ass in Chair.* If I feel stuck, or I feel like walking away from the computer, I look up and he is there, hard at work. And I will not let him beat me. No, I'll get back to it.

But, if I'm really being honest, all his literary influence on my life is, to me, secondary. Forget *literary* friend—he's my *friend.* He's my son's godfather. He gave me away at my wedding. He and my husband have weekly movie nights.

In another lifetime, we'd stay up all night drinking bourbon while one of us cried and complained (me), or speak very elegantly and poetically about how our current misfortunes influenced our growth as human beings (Jeff). When I introduced him to guys I was dating, he said, "He was very nice. What about that guy Christopher?"

In a lifetime before that, we sweated over graduate theses. When I introduced him to guys I was dating, he said, "He was very nice. But he looks sort of like a Troll. You know those Troll dolls? With the...hair?"

Before *that* was the fateful night where, after he walked me home from a late night class, and I took a purposely long time looking for my keys until finally, finally drumming up the courage to look up at him and say, "Would you like to have dinner with me this weekend?" I was twenty years old. I'd recently broken up with my high school boyfriend. I was brand new to the big city, brand new to my adult life, and Jeff had walked me home after every night class for nearly a year.

"I'd love to have dinner with you!" he said. "You know I'm gay, right?"

Looking back on it, this was the moment where I learned that there are different kinds of love. It's a long, complicated novel, not a three-minute pop song. And for me, that's what Oscar and Veronica is about: letting go long enough to move onto the next chapter.

One final thought: I recently read that Emerson owned the property at Walden Pond and gave it to Thoreau to build his cabin.

Jeff? Are you reading this? Hurry up and buy some land so I can build myself a cabin.

I'd prefer this land to be in Spain.

But I'm not picky.

CAN I BUY YOU A DRINK?

It took me a while to understand that Can I buy you a drink? doesn't actually mean Can I buy you a drink? but rather Can I buy permission to sit with you while you drink that drink, during which time a romantic and/or sexual interest might spark, at which point I'll offer to buy more drinks until I get one of the following, depending on where we both are intellectually, emotionally, and developmentally at this particular moment in time: 1) a phone number so I can contact you for dinner and conversation, 'cause I think you're really interesting and who knows where this might go? 2) consensual sexy time in the women's bathroom, sweaty and sticky and thrilling, because sometimes both parties want that with every fiber of their being, but please note that the operative word in that sentence is *consensual*, so ask, motherfucker, and 3) after you say "no thanks" to another drink and "no thanks" to a ride home and "I don't think so" when he asks for your number, because naive as you are at 21, you're still smart enough not to give your contact information to a guy who knocks back three whiskies to your every one vodka tonic, to a guy already slurring his words, to a guy who says, "Oh, come on, honey," like you owe him something, so what you do is this: put a $20 down on the bar, get your coat, and leave.

Late as it is, walking out of the dim-dark bar onto Addison Avenue is like flipping a light switch: bars and people and laughing and tipsy and music and life. It's January in Chicago and you can see your breath as you walk, a few blocks down that main drag, and then a few blocks down the side street where you parked your car.

Fifteen years later and you still don't park on side streets.

Snap your fingers—that's how fast a city street goes silent. The lights and noise of Addison are gone now; in their place are rows of residential three-flats with darkened windows. All you can hear is your own breath, your own heartbeat, your own footsteps in the snow as you hurry towards your car with its wonderful, wonderful heater and then, from a behind you: "Hey! Honey! Wait up!"

Fifteen years later and the fear is still paralyzing.

Slowly, you look over your shoulder, and there he is, in the middle of the empty street. "Wait up!" he calls again, the snow crunching underneath his feet, coming closer, closer, and fuck it, you turn and run, your breath and heartbeat and footsteps racing towards your car with its wonderful, wonderful locks, and behind you he's yelling, "I said wait up!" and "Why the fuck are you running?" and "I'm not going to fucking rape you!"

Can I buy you a drink?

I'm not going to fucking rape you.

You're at your car, in your car, locked in your car, and then he's there, too, rattling the door handle, fists pounding the window, but you're already driving away, and now, 15 years later, you never walk to your car without your keys in your hand, and now, 15 years later, you're still overwhelmed with gratitude that you were spared what so many women are not, and now, 15 years later, when someone asks if they can buy you a drink, your first thought isn't, "No thanks, I'm married," or "No thanks, I can buy my own," or "No thanks, although I'm sure you're very nice—nothing at all like that guy from that night who's lived for so long uninvited in my memory." No, your first thought is this:

What will I owe you?

WE ARE FINE

FOUR YEARS AGO, I leaned over the bathtub to pick up my then one-year-old son, and something in my lower back snapped. It happened so fast: one second I'm bent right-angled at the waist, arms around my wet, slippery tank of a kid; the next second— flat on the floor. I couldn't move. Even the *idea* of moving was an impossibility. I lay there for nearly forty-five minutes—never in my life have I been as helpless—until finally, I worked myself into an awkward push-up position and slowly, slowly, military-crawled to the phone in the next room. I remember the pain made me see white—a blizzard on the backs of my eyelids.

Over the years, I've told this story to chiropractors, physical therapists, and yoga instructors. "Do you have injuries I should be aware of?" they ask, and again and again and again, I begin: "I was leaning over the bathtub to pick up my son, and something in my lower back..." For every time I've told it, every time I've relived it as part of understanding my own body, there is one part I always leave out:

I dropped him.

My beautiful, perfect tank of a little boy.

I dropped him.

Around a year later, my physical therapist cleared me for yoga. I will never forget those first months, approaching my mat as though it were an active volcano. On it, I might hurt myself again; half an inch in the wrong direction, and all this work, all this fragile healing could snap. "It's not safe," I said to my best friend, Dia. She'd been practicing yoga for years and dealing with me for longer.

"What's not safe?" she said. "That?" indicating my mat, "or this?" indicating my head.

One morning, my teacher, Francine, guided us into Cobra Pose, and I started to shake. This always happened when I was asked to lie face-down. Too many times, I'd been unable to get up afterwards—my lower back seizing—and then, like always, I'd be back on that bathroom floor with my son lying next to me, his little eyes wide with shock. This image had become my *drishti*, my focus, my intention—for the life of me, I couldn't shake it— and in the midst of my rising panic, Francine's voice cut through like a life raft. "What if it isn't a struggle?" she asked. "What if you welcome the fear?"

I'm not a crier, but that day I couldn't stop. I lay on my back, tears leaking sideways into my ears. Francine held my head in her hands, her calm, lovely voice continuing to guide the rest of the class in and out of poses while quietly holding space with me.

I'm trying to understand what is in my body and what is in my head. Sometimes, there is pain, a blizzard behind my eyes, and I name it: *this* hurts. I ripped something, pulled something, pushed myself too far. Other times, I think: *Wait. That's not pain. It's fear.* And then I think: *Is there a difference?*

Recently, I went to see a massage therapist for the first time, a woman named Dana who Dia had been recommending for years. When I arrived at her studio, she gave me a printed diagram of a body and asked me to mark the areas I wanted her to focus on. I circled the lower back. Then I circled the head, wrote the word FEAR next to it in all caps, and handed it back to her.

She glanced at what I'd done, invited me to sit, and listened for over an hour. "I'm too young for this," I told her, and "What if it happens again?" and "I dropped him." Something magical happened then: explaining it all to Dana allowed me to explain it to myself.

This healing of the body begins with words.

Dia is a yoga instructor now in San Francisco. A few months ago I went to visit and joined her class, unrolling my mat in the back of the room. We're friends now, that mat and I—four years of careful movement, cautious breathing, stopping when my body says stop.

Dia leads us through Sun Salutations, balance poses, and Breath of Joy, and in all of it, I am present, clear, fast, and free. Then she tells us it's time to play with handstands, and just like that—I'm out. I slide back into Child's Pose. The rest of the class lifts their legs in the air with various levels of success, and like always, I remain still. I protect myself. I breathe: *inhale, exhale, inhale, exhale.* Usually, teachers leave me alone. They've heard my story: "I was leaning over the bathtub, and something in my lower back..." But this time, I feel a gentle tap.

"Let's try that handstand!" Dia says.

I shake my head no, and she squats down next to me. "Do you trust me?" she asks.

I think of that day on the bathroom floor, my back bones snapping like kindling. I think of the creative writing classes I teach, and how, on the first day, we talk about what it means to trust your instincts. Most of all, I think about Dia. For twenty years, she's been there, telling me what I most need to hear about my jobs, my relationships, my fears, my body.

"I trust you," I tell her.

And then, for the first time in my life, I stand on my hands.

In my life outside of my body, I help people tell their stories. Recently, I had the privilege of working with a yoga teacher named Jen. She wrote about a student who cried in class. About holding this woman's head in her hands. About holding space. "Does it happen often?" I asked, thinking of that day with Francine.

She said, "All the time."

So much work I've done, this fragile healing. One morning, years ago, I lay on the bathroom floor unable to move with my then one-year-old son next to me; both of us dropped from an impossible height. For a single second, maybe two, his eyes were wide in shock. Then, he was up, naked and giggling. For forty-five minutes I listened to him run around the apartment, playing with toys, toddling on perfect, fat little legs—he was *fine*. Hitting the floor was one of a thousand moments in his short life where something could have gone one way, but didn't.

We are *fine*.

For the moments when things aren't fine, Francine has suggested a mantra. I am new to this mantra thing; still finding its place on my tongue in a way that feels authentic. I try because Francine gave it to me, and I trust her, the same way I trust Dia to lift my feet off the ground, or Dana to place her hands on my lower back and help me find myself.

Netti netti netti.

It means *Not That.*

I am broken—*netti netti netti.* I am afraid—*netti netti netti.* I am silent—*netti netti netti.* And what if it wasn't a struggle?

DRAGONS SO HUGE

My friend Bobby Biedrzycki and I wrote this piece
together about an experience we shared.

BOBBY: First off, I think it's important for you to know that this is not a story about endings, although there will be talk of endings. And that this is not a story about addiction, although there will be lots of talk of addiction. And this is definitely not a story about suicide, although there will be talk of suicide. Because most importantly, beyond all the things I just mentioned and beyond just about everything else, this is a story about miracles.

MEGAN: October 2009, the last night of 2nd Story's very first West Coast tour. I was sitting alone on the back patio at the Bookwalter Vineyard in Washington State, drinking a hot-off-the-presses Pinot Noir out of a very fancy glass, which for some magical reason always makes it taste better. Behind me, inside Bookwalter's jam-packed wine bar, I heard Seeking Wonderland, 2nd Story's house band, and the happy, tipsy chatter of our post-show audience. We kicked ass that night. We kicked ass all three nights; opening the Wordstock Lit Festival in Portland and two sold-out shows in the vineyard, surrounded on all sides by miles of grapes and above us—stars. I remember watching them like a movie. In the city, you can never see them, but out there, it was one of those moments where you understand how enormous the world really is.

That's when Bobby sat next to me. He's a storyteller. He's also my friend. He's also, I had recently learned—learned, in fact, one week earlier, the day before we flew to Portland—an alcoholic. Friends of ours reading this will wonder how I didn't know, how I didn't see. I've asked myself that same question, and every answer sucks: I didn't want to see. I was busy, we weren't that close, we never hung out at night, he didn't care what I thought, and he damn sure didn't want to change—at least not until that last night of our tour, when he sat next to me under the stars.

He was holding a drink.

After the week we'd just had, he had the nerve to sit down next to me with a glass of fucking wine. I looked at it—not at him, just the glass—and you know what he said? He said:

Bobby: "I'm done."

Megan: He held it up, studying the contents like a map.

Bobby: "I'm not gonna drink anymore."

Megan: Maybe some of you have heard those words before. Hell, maybe you've said them. Last drink ever? Riiiight. That'd be a fucking miracle.

Bobby: So where do you begin a story about miracles? Well,

this one starts at the bottom. In October 2009, I was suicidal. That Tuesday morning before we left for Portland, I found myself standing on a train platform in Edgewater, ready to die. This did not happen overnight. I had been struggling for years with depression, anxiety, and a long time addiction to drugs and alcohol. A close friend had died the year before; I had found him in the apartment we shared, and the image of his dead body was burned into my mind. Life had been getting progressively hazy, but right then, standing on that train platform, life was beyond hazy; life was pitch black.

Megan: That same morning, I woke up to voicemails: *Bobby didn't show up for rehearsal, didn't show up to our meeting, didn't show up to teach his morning class.* No one knew where he was, and in 24 horribly short hours, I was supposed to get on a plane with Bobby, three other storytellers, and a nine-piece band. Our artistic director, Amanda, had gone to Portland ahead to rent cars, and before she'd left, she'd said, "Just promise you'll get them on the plane; in their seats, belts fastened."

If I could find Bobby, I'd have belted him to the fucking wings.

Bobby: I'd been on a three-day drug and alcohol bender brought on by increasing anxiety attacks, or had I been coming off a three-day anxiety attack brought on by drugs and alcohol? When dealing with these two afflictions it's often hard to tell which is which.

Those of you out there that have battled any or all of these issues would probably agree that suicide is always an option. For me though, it was usually a ways down the line though. *If this, this, this, or this doesn't work out, then I can always just kill myself.* I know it sounds grim, but when you live with it for long enough it becomes your reality. But on that day before we left for Portland, suicide was no longer E, F, or G; suicide was plan A-ish. I'd been staying with Amanda and her boyfriend, Nic, and that morning, when I left their condo, I was pretty sure I was going to kill myself.

Megan: By the time our friend Julia called, I was wrecked.

"Did Bobby call?"—we said at the same time.

"No."—we said at the same time.

And then, cautiously, she asked if I had keys to Amanda's. At the time, I ran workshops for 2nd Story out of her and Nic's living room. "Sure," I told Julia, "I have keys," and then she said it: "You know what this weekend is, right?" Suddenly, none of it mattered. Who cared if we got on the plane. Who cared about our stupid tour, our stupid stories. The year before—almost to the date—Bobby had walked into his friend's bedroom and found him dead.

Now, Bobby was missing. And the only one with house keys was me.

[pause]

Bobby: Standing on that train platform—

Megan: Standing in front of Bobby's bedroom door—

Bobby: I wasn't...scared—

Megan: I was so *scared*—

Bobby: I actually felt kind of calm.

Megan: I'd already looked everywhere else: the living room, dining room, kitchen, bedroom, two offices, five closets, walk-in pantry, behind two shower curtains, sunroom, back porch, garage; each step an attempt to avoid his bedroom, because honestly—

Bobby: I still hadn't decided if I was going to do it.

Megan: If he was going to do it, that'd be the place.

Bobby: I mean, you don't decide until you *decide*, right?

[pause]

Megan: I reached for the doorknob—

Bobby: The tracks began to rumble—

Megan: It was like watching a movie—

Bobby: Getting louder—

Megan: When you already know what's going to happen—

Bobby: Getting closer—

Megan: And you yell *No, don't do it!* at the characters like they can hear you—

Bobby: And as it pulled into the station, I had this thought: Nic and Amanda just purchased the condo I was living in. If I killed myself right here on these L tracks, a block away, they would never escape it. It would ruin their home, their neighborhood, even their lives. Now there are probably a million ways to psychoanalyze this thinking process, but in the moment it was just a fact: I can't kill myself here, Nic and Amanda live here.

[pause]

I have to do it somewhere else.

[pause]

Megan: I opened the door—

Bobby: I boarded the train—

Megan: And saw an empty room. I thought I would feel relieved, but the thing about suicide is that once you've *decided*, you've decided.

There are a thousand bedrooms in this city.

A hundred L stops.

[pause]

I sat on Bobby's bed for a long time, then I left him a voicemail: "Please, just call me... love you."

Bobby: When I arrived at 95th street, as far south as the Red Line went, I checked my phone. I'd had it on silent, and when I looked it was full of messages and texts. I picked it up and heard a voicemail from Megan.

Megan: "Please, just call me... love you."

Bobby: If there's a moment I decided I wasn't going to kill my-self, at least not right then, and at least not on that train, this was the moment.

Megan: You never realize the power of your own words: "Please, just call me ... I love you."

Bobby: And within seconds of making that decision I went di-rectly to a bar and got blackout drunk.

Megan: The next morning, face-to-face at the airport, my words were... not so nice. I yelled a lot—about the money our organiza-tion had sunk into this trip; the students he'd left waiting in the hallway; about standing in front of his bedroom door, and how I'd never get those minutes of my life back.
 Any of you ever talk shop with an alcoholic?
 He didn't hear a word I said.

Bobby: The word alcoholic came at me from everywhere. Within an hour of landing in Portland, I got a call from the college where I teach, telling me I was suspended; my friends weighed in on my voicemail and to my face; and finally, my longtime therapist, Bea—a woman I trusted more than anyone on the planet—called long distance to say she'd seen enough.
 "You're an alcoholic and a drug addict. This is my diagnosis."
 I sat on a park bench outside our hotel, listening to her lay it out: she would no longer treat me for depression and anxiety, no more medications would be prescribed, and no more letters

written to employers my behalf. She would not be my doctor if I did not go to rehab.

I couldn't believe it. Through tears and screams I told her she was breaking our trust, that I was not going to rehab, and that she was going to keep treating me, or I'd sue her for malpractice. When she held strong, I told her to stay out of my life forever, then I hung up and sat on that bench, crying—right up until our tour manager called, telling me it was time to head to the theater. My heart nearly stopped. I had not thought about performing in days. I knew the piece, but I wasn't sure I could actually get up on stage and do it.

Megan: He got up on stage and fucking brought the house down. The show was at The Bagdad, this old, beautiful theatre with a huge balcony—seats around 500, I'd guess? That night, it was packed for the opening night of Wordstock, and when Bobby performed, the crowd went crazy.

Bobby: Honestly? I don't remember any of that.

Megan: His story was about sitting in a strip club and seeing— on the pole, dancing—the first girl he ever slept with. Right? He was fifteen years old, sooo in love with her, and—get this—she asks him to *get her pregnant so she could trap her boyfriend.* And Bobby did it! He slept with her!

Bobby: She was *so beautiful.* And I was Catholic! The only way you get to have sex when you're Catholic is for procreation!

Megan: *Anyhow*—it was this crazy, awkward, improbable situa-

tion, but right at the end of the story, Bobby asks the audience—
he asks *us*—to consider: "How a simple blip in the matrix—"

Bobby: My *sperm not* connecting with her egg—

Megan: "Allowed our lives to instead diverge."

I'd heard Bobby tell that story a thousand times, and every
time that line takes me right out of the strip club and into my
own life: *how a simple blip in the matrix allowed me to diverge.*
A blip, and I moved to Chicago; a blip, and I met my husband; a
blip, and I'm talking to you. But back then, sitting in the balcony
at The Bagdad Theater watching 500 people hang on Bobby's every word, I wondered if this could, for him, be a moment where
his life would diverge.

Bobby: The next morning we drove six hours to Bookwalter
Vineyard in Washington State and did two more shows on con-
secutive nights. Most of that was also a blur until the last night,
when I sat down next to Megan, drinking her hot-off-the-presses Pinot Noir out of a very fancy glass. And it was there, staring out over acres and acres of grapes, that it happened. Call it
a spiritual experience, or the hand of God, or the universe, or
whatever you like, but I had a moment. It happened this fast: one
minute I very much believed that I would drink forever, and the
next (snap), I knew I was done.

Megan: Have you ever been in the presence of a miracle?

Bobby: It was like remembering something—

Megan: I didn't know it at the time, of course—

Bobby: Where I'd left my keys—

Megan: At the time I doubted every word out of his mouth.

Bobby: Or a book I'd hidden somewhere—

Megan: But now? Three years later?—

Bobby: It was over.

Megan: —after watching him, every day, slay dragons so huge and deadly and terrifying they could level this city?

Bobby: I turned to Megan, stunned by the words that were about to fall out of my mouth: "I'm done."

Megan: He held up the glass, studying the contents like a map.

Bobby: "I'm not gonna drink anymore."

Megan: And then he put it down. We sat there, watching the stars—all those tiny little blips in the matrix. In the city, you can never see them, but out there? It was one of those moments where you understand how miraculous the world really is.

THE ART OF THE EXCUSE

ONCE I WAS COOL, things would be easy. I'd know how to put on eyeliner correctly. I'd know what music to like. I'd know the right thing to say at parties. My friend Jeff sticks Post-it notes on his bookshelves that say "MEGAN GO TALK TO SOMEONE," because at his parties, I stand there, nursing the same plastic cup of Maker's Mark and reading all his book titles. Then I count how many *the*'s were in all the titles. Then I count the *e*'s. Then it's time to go home—alone. I haven't spoken to anyone—again. Because whenever I try, I'd panic—this choking, squeezing electricity wrapping my limbs like vines.

Once I got a boyfriend, I would not have to have sex with people I shouldn't be having sex with; unless, of course, I wanted to have sex with them, which is sometimes the case. Sometimes we're lonely. Sometimes we're drunk. Sometimes, it's the only way we know how to heal. Other times, we're bored. *So* bored. Bored out of our fucking skulls with the day-in/day-out, nutsandbolts grind of *go here, do this, drink that, did you get that file? I sent it to you, did you get it? Please read the entire email. Please don't click reply all. How's about I Google that for you? How's about I cancel the meeting at the exact time it's supposed to begin? How's about I do the thing that is my job, and you do the thing that is your job! Then all the jobs will be done! It's like magic!*

And sometimes, we just like sex.

Once I lost weight, I'd be able to wear tank tops. I could finally get the tattoo I want across my shoulders because my arms would be nice; not ripped like Linda Hamilton in *Terminator II*, or Angela Bassett in anything (Dear Angela Bassett: I love you. Please be my best friend, my personal trainer, and my mentor in all things), but *nice*—enough to wear tank tops, to show off my tattoos, to not be anxious about mirrors, cameras, camera phones, or cute girls who tell me how much they love my hair and/or purse and/or shoes.

Once I finished my MFA, I'd have time to read all the books I was supposed to be reading. I'd have so much extra time!

Once I finished my MFA, I'd have time to write the book I said I was writing. I'd have so much fucking time.

Once I got a book contract, I'd be *set.*

Once I got a boyfriend, I'd have someone to put in my window air conditioner. Most of the stuff that gets attributed to guys—stuff like power tools, carburetors, guns, ants—I can do all that by myself. But summers in Chicago? They're brutal; brutal and gorgeous, like we're all walking around in a sexy, steamy Def Leppard video, and no matter how much Gloria Steinem I've read, no matter how much bell hooks, those window air conditioners are still fucking *heavy*.

Once I've read enough bell hooks, I can start to examine my own privilege. Also: Audre Lorde. And W.E.B. DuBois. Baldwin. I need to educate my own damn self about the experience of race in my own damn country. I need to acknowledge what I've received that I haven't earned. I need to own that it won't be a one-stop shop, but rather an ongoing conversation I'll be having with myself for probably always. I should probably take a class on critical race theory; gender theory, too. *Then*, I can get started. *Then*, I can dig in. *Then*, I can look in the mirror. *Then*.

Once my CV was as good as his CV, I could apply. All I needed was more workshops. And panels. And awards and honors and service. Oh, and writing. Once I had time to get some writing done, I'd publish it and put it on my CV, and then it would be as good as his and I could apply.

Once I formatted my CV, I could apply for that teaching gig. *NEED GOOD FONTS.*

Once I got a teaching gig, I wouldn't have to wait tables anymore because what I'd be paid as an educator would be waaaay more than what I make serving pancakes. Plus, I'd have health insurance! All teachers get health insurance, right?

Once I had health insurance, I could get _____ taken care of.

Once I hit that elusive point in my freelance career where I no longer had to accept pro bono work to establish my credentials, I wouldn't have to say yes to everything. I could be selective. Only projects I cared about. The ones that made my blood boil. *Passion*—that's the word.

Once that happened, *for love* and *for money* would mean the same thing.

Once I paid off my loans, I'd be able to start saving for retirement. An IRA, right? Or something. I don't want to eat cat food when I'm old.

Once he was no longer my student, I'd be able to think about him in that way.

Once we'd been together for a month, I'd be able to trust him.

I'd know after a month, right?

Two months?

Three?

Once we moved in together, I'd be able to trust him.

Once he proposed, I'd be able to trust him.

Once we got married, things would be easy. Everybody would stop asking us when we were going to get married.

Once we owned a place, I could have central air conditioning. I could have central air conditioning and built-in bookshelves that go up to the ceiling, like something you'd see on bookshelfporn.com. Maybe there'd be a ladder up to the top, on wheels so you could slide it around. My friend Maggie and I were looking at bookshelves with ladders just now on the Internet, and it said they were made by the "skilled hands of German artisans." Not gonna lie: that got me a little hot.

Once we owned a place, its property value would increase and in a few years we'd be able to sell it and buy something a little bigger. It's what they call "building escrow." It's what they call "being an adult." It's what they call "The American Dream."

Once we owned a place, things would be easy. The developers would *totally* have put the roof on correctly. We wouldn't have to redo it in the first few years! We wouldn't have to take out an enormous loan to pay for it! I wouldn't think our condo board treasurer was joking when she told us how much it was going to cost! I wouldn't have laughed like crazy, and everyone wouldn't have looked at me the way that they looked at me.

Also: the housing market totally wouldn't crash. That shit never happens.

Once I got pregnant; once the window in the little plastic stick turned pink; once I took a second test to be sure, and that one turned pink, too; once I called the doctor to verify, and she couldn't see me 'til later in the day, and I drank like nine bottles of water in the coffee shop next door to her office, so when I finally did the pee test it came out all water, and she couldn't tell, so she drew blood; once she called the next day and said, yes, it was true—all those months, and now it was true; once I showed the stick to my husband, and he put both fists in the air and yelled, "I am the captain of the swim team!"; once I could stop counting days on that ovulation calendar and stop locking myself in the bathroom for the fast, private cry I allowed myself month after month when my period came; once we knew that the baby was a baby, that it was healthy and growing and normal; once this thing I so desperately wanted had finally, finally, finally happened—I would *totally* know what to do next.

Once he was born?

I'd know what to do then, too.

Once they got the tumor out of me, I would travel more.

Once we paid off the condo, we'd be able to travel more. New Zealand. Tokyo. Melbourne. Maybe somewhere with a pristine white beach and pristine blue water, like you see in movies or television commercials. By then I'll be in my seventies, but who gives a shit?

Once we sold the condo, my husband could quit his job and blog full-time.

Once we did a short-sale on the condo, I could quit the one job I didn't like and only work the three jobs I did like.

Once I got a second book contract, I could quit all the jobs and write full-time. One more book contract and I'd be *set.*

Once we walked away from the condo, I'd be able to have a desk. We'd rent a new place—rent, not buy; I'll slit my wrists before I'll buy again—with lots of space, and I'd have somewhere to work that's all my own. I could hang up my own stuff! Art and postcards and Post-it notes with ideas and plans. Plans! I could actually plan out a book instead of piecing together all the little bits I write on the L, or stuck in traffic on Lakeshore Drive, or in the coffee shop, or while my kid is napping. While my kid is napping, I'll go sit at my desk. I'll be able to think. No to-do lists, no distractions, just me. Just...*shhhhhhh.*

Once my kid went down for a nap, I'd read all the books I was supposed to be reading.

Once my kid went down for a nap, I'd write the book I said I was writing.

Once my kid stopped napping, I'd be fucked.

Once my kid started school, I'd have time. I'd have so much fucking time. Time to sleep. To travel. To think more fully about my teaching, instead of during the five minutes before and after class. To order those special seeds for the vertical window garden we backed on Kickstarter. To read more books. To buy new pants. To go to yoga more often. To get my work done during the day so I could be more fully present with my son: going for walks, building Legos, discussing the part in *Honey I Shrunk the Kids* where the ant dies, discussing the part in *Symphony City* where the girl gets lost, discussing everything.

Once my back healed, I could go to yoga.

Once I lost weight, I could start yoga.

Once I could fit into those cute Lululemon pants, I could start yoga.

Once we got my meds right, maybe I'd lose weight. Maybe I'd be able to sleep. When my doctor first told me my THS levels, she said, "I can't believe you didn't know something was wrong! Aren't you *exhausted?*"

I told her I have four jobs.

I told her I have a five-year-old kid.

I told her I was trying to write.

I told her something about "America in This Day and Age," but I'm not sure what I meant.

I told her that I was lucky.

Once we got our credit back—

Fuck it.

Once I had more followers on Twitter—

Fuck it.

Once _____ was dead, I'll be able to write about _____.

Once I found those shoes that were re-pinned a gazillion times on Pinterest, but the link didn't take you to a place where you could actually buy them, everything would be okay.

Once we paid off the IRS, everything would be okay.

Once I have a day off, everything will be okay. I'll take my little boy to the beach. We'll lie in the sand and stare at the sky. He'll ask me a thousand questions, many of which I won't be able to answer. He'll say, "But you're the mommy! Mommies are supposed to know everything!" and I'll say that all I can do is the best I can, and he'll pat my shoulder and say, "It's okay, Mommy." He'll say, "You're still the best mommy." He'll say, "We can always Google it."

Once I finish a draft of this essay, I'll know what I'm trying to say. "I don't know what I think until I see what I say"—E.M. Forster wrote that. Or maybe it was Flannery O'Connor? I don't know—I'll Google it. Then I'll check Facebook. And Twitter. And Instagram. I'll see if anything new is on Colossal or Brainpicker, maybe read the day's essay at The Rumpus. Inevitably, I'll get up to make tea. Once I make tea, I'll be able to finish this essay. I'll know what I'm trying to say.

My oven is schkeevy. I should clean it.

Shit. Some of the schkeeve got on the floor. I should clean it.

The kitchen floor is connected to the floor in the rest of the house; I should clean it—I can finish this essay tomorrow. It'll still be here tomorrow, right?

I'll still be here tomorrow.

NICE

PICTURE IT: 1998, I'm 23 years old and sitting on the front couch at Tuman's, which back then was called The Alcohol Abuse Center. Anybody remember the Alcohol Abuse Center? Right?! The most miserable, disgraceful, health-code violating, awesome fucking dive bar in Chicago? Seriously. Fireside Bowl, Liar's Club, The Mutiny on Western where I once saw a guy pee in the corner pocket of the pool table—all five-star fine dining compared to Tuman's in the '90s. Tuman's in the '90s had Old Style on tap for two bucks. Tuman's in the '90s had a jukebox with Fugazi, Motorhead, and John fucking Philip fucking Sousa. Tuman's in the '90s had a motto: "We service and install all hangovers," and believe you me, they did the job. I lost whole chunks of my early twenties to this place, with a notable exception being that one awful night on the front couch, when Jackson Jackman[1] told me I was JUST. TOO. NICE.

Jackson fucking Jackman. At the time, he played guitar for a band called The Lasertags.[2] Have you heard of The Lasertags?

No? *Shocking.* They described themselves as Jane's Addiction meets Captain Beefheart meets Godspeed You! Black Emperor, which to me sounded like a lot of fucking noise. But it didn't matter because Jackson Jackman had a strip of hair that fell over his eyes; he wore very tight, ironic T-shirts from the kid's section at Salvation Army; and when he played guitar, he'd open his mouth, like he was singing the chords. Also, he had the phrase "Everything was beautiful and nothing hurt" tattooed across his chest,[3] which—since I loved Vonnegut—was so totally a sign. Who cared that he didn't have a job. Who cared that my friend Dia regularly saw him passed out in Swank Frank at the corner of Milwaukee and Damen. Who cared that he went on "tour" with The Lasertags, would call from the "road" to say how much he missed me; and one night, after an especially emotional phone call from "Philly," I went to Tuman's to have a late drink and there he was. Sitting at the bar. With a girl.

Everything, most definitely, was not *beautiful.*

Everything, most definitely, *hurt.*

He took me to the couch and explained that he was going to tell me, really he was, but you know how sometimes, when you have to do something, you keep putting it off? Like getting an oil change, for example?

I said, "Am I the oil change in this scenario?"

And he said, "Oh, Megan. You're JUST. TOO—" and yes, of course, I knew what was coming; not because I'd *heard* it before, but because I'd *said* it. I'd told my first boyfriend, Brad, that he was *too nice for me,* because I was scared to say I didn't love him back. I told my friend Kelly that she *deserved someone nicer,* because I was too confused to say I knew that I was straight. I told Andy, the guy I didn't know how to get rid of, that he was *just too nice*, because I didn't have the wisdom or the language or the balls to say, "I don't have any idea what I am looking for in a boyfriend or a lover or a partner, but I do know, without a shadow of a doubt, that you are not it."

None of that has anything to do with *nice*.

Now, granted, I'm no expert in linguistics, but somewhere along the line, NICE got a pretty bad rap. We use it when the truth is too messy, too complicated. We use it as a replacement for *needy. Weak. Boring. Unattractive. Prudish*—prudish for chrissakes, like that makes any sense! Personally, I think having a partner fulfill all your crazy, wild, innermost sexual fantasies is pretty goddamn nice! But the point, the point is this: how has this single, simple, lovely word come to represent anything besides its actual dictionary definition of being a decent fucking human being?

The "fucking" part isn't really in the dictionary.

The decent part is.

So is kindness. Honesty. Compassion. Generosity.

All things this world could use a little more of, don't you think?

Picture it: 2012, I'm 37 years old, standing in the lobby of Pump It Up, which if you haven't had the pleasure, is a ginormous indoor arena of inflatable bouncy castles where your children turn into foaming, rabid animals. I'm hand-in-hand with my four-year-old son, who's already twitching with excitement and sugar and helium balloons. We're here for his school friend's birthday party, one of twenty birthday parties happening that moment simultaneously, which means there are—no joke—*hundreds* of batshit crazy children everywhere, and all of them are jumping. My imagination, usually my greatest asset as a writer, is now, as a parent, my greatest liability because I can see, almost cinematically, all their little skulls cracking together—the massive ER bills, the missing person reports, parenting bloggers writhing in judgment—and in the midst of it all, my little boy tugs on my hand.

"It's okay, Mommy," he says. "You can let go. I promise I'll be nice."

Here's what he means when he says nice: I'll say please and thank you. I won't cut in line. No biting, no kicking, no hitting. I'll let the littler kids go up the ladder first, and if they need help, I'll help. When you ask me something, I'll listen.

I'll listen.

Let's imagine what might happen if—right now, in this very second of reading these words—we reclaim the idea of nice and what it has the potential to achieve. Maybe buy the person sitting next to you a drink; they might really need it. The next time you go through a toll, pay the fare of the person behind you. Chicago, if you get back to your car before the parking ticket runs out of time, give the sticker to the person waiting for your spot. Might make their day, and we could all use our day made, right? *Listen.* Let the person you're talking to finish their sentence. Don't use the time they're talking to figure out what you're going to say next. If someone is being a jackass, step up. You overhear something a little racist, a little sexist, a little homophobic, call that shit out. It's on you. It's on us. Be NICE. Back something interesting on Kickstarter later; that's someone's idea, someone's dream, someone's pulsing heart. College teachers: Don't call your students *kids.* They're not kids. Also: don't start sentences with *Kids today,* because then I'll have to vomit all over you, and that wouldn't be very nice of me, now would it? Before you hit send on that email—you know the one I'm talking about; the one where you're a little passive-aggressive and maybe even used the caps lock key—take a lap or two around the house. It'll give you a second to think things through, calm down a little bit, and even log some steps on your Fitbit! Win-win! Also winning: *sleep.* Sleep on it. Sleep on everything, always. Before you make the shitty anonymous comment on the Internet, consider the fact that there's a real person on the other end, reading your words and feeling that punch to the chest. Can we use a phrase other than, "I didn't like it," or "It sucked," to talk about movies or TV shows or music or books or art? Somebody *made that.* In fact, can we put a moratorium on the word *suck* entirely unless in reference to lollipops, Dyson, or super-hot sex? Be honest in your assessment, be authentic in your language, but be nice. BE FUCKING NICE. If all this sounds too hard, too impossible, then may I respectfully suggest you put down this book and go take a vacation. I give you permission. Go online and buy a ticket to somewhere: a quiet beach, a noisy jazz fest, even the hotel down the street for a night if you need some sleep. Sleep is a major ingredient for niceness. If someone cuts you off in traffic, let it go, it doesn't matter in the grand, glowing scheme of you and me and all of us breathing a little easier. Above all else, when you get home tonight, write these words on a Post-it note:

BE KIND, FOR EVERYONE IS FIGHTING A HARD BATTLE.[4]

Stick that Post-it to your bathroom mirror and read it every morning, before you leave the house:

BE KIND.

BE KIND.

BE KIND.

Footnotes:

1. Not his real name, duh.

2. Not their real name, duh.

3. This part is real, but I'm not worried about giving him away because I'd wager tons of people have this same tattoo.

4. This has been attributed to Plato, Philo of Alexandria, and John Watson aka Ian MacLaren. My thanks to all those guys.

THIS IS SCARY AND HERE I GO

A COUPLE of lifetimes ago, I got a teaching gig at a very fancy university. This place had *history*. It had hauntingly beautiful gothic architecture, a state-of-the-art library that went back centuries, and this strange and wonderful thing called a quad where students sat in the grass reading Aristotle aloud to each other and discussing how their actions defined their true selves. It was in that quad, on my way to my very first class, that the panic kicked in: *What am I doing here? How did I get here? Am I a total fraud?*

I got out my cell phone and called my friend Jeff. When he picked up, I said, "I think I'm a fraud."

The reception was shitty.

"You're a what?" he said.

"A fraud," I said.

"A frog?"

"A FRAUD."

"YOU'RE A FROG?"

"FRAUD. F-R-A-U-D."

Some students were looking at me, yelling into my phone in their lovely, lovely quad. We were all so young. We had so much to learn from each other. I took a big breath and thought of what I'd gone through to be there. I thought, it's either *This is scary; I'm going home*, or *This is scary; here I go.* I thought I might choke on all my beautiful, terrifying gratitude.

"Actually, I did say frog," I told Jeff. "I'm a frog."

"YOU'RE A WHAT?"

"I'm a motherfucking *frog.*"

There's so much second-guessing, so much doubt. When I recognize the feeling, I try to stand very still, and breathe, and think of what I've gone through to get here. How profoundly grateful I am. How this is scary and here I go.

I am a motherfucking frog.

AN ESSAY ABOUT ESSAYS

IN THE INTRODUCTORY PARAGRAPH to this essay about essays, I will tell you that you don't need an introductory paragraph, at least not of the 1) *topic sentence* 2) *structural methodology* 3) *thesis statement* variety that we were all taught in high school. What you do need is *That Thing*; maybe a question, a fear, or a fury. It makes your blood boil. It's all you can talk about when you sit down with your friends over a glass of wine or two or five, or maybe you can't talk about it with anyone, just your own heart, alone with the impossible architecture of words. As Cheryl Strayed wrote in her introduction to *The Best American Essays 2013*, "Behind every good essay is an author with a savage desire to know more about what is already known." I want to talk about essays. I don't have a topic sentence or a thesis statement, just a savage desire to know.

•

In the first body paragraph paragraph of this essay about essays, I will talk about how the writing of essays is currently taught: five paragraphs—introductory paragraph, three paragraphs of support, conclusion. Sound familiar? I'd wager we all learned this particular form, and yes, I think it's vital to know how to organize our thoughts and back up an argument, however, the assumption that there's only one way to do so is increasingly problematic, especially in light of this country's current testing culture. We're not teaching writing as a course of exploration and discovery, a way to follow your own passion and curiosity and then share that passion and curiosity with others; we're teaching writing as a way to get a grade. Every year, thousands of high school students across the United States and other countries sit for the three hours and forty-five minutes required to take the SAT. Twenty-five of those minutes are spent writing an essay that's graded on a scale of 1-6 by two independent readers who, according to the Collegeboard website, score in a holistic manner, taking into account such aspects as complexity of thought, substantiality of development, and facility with language, which is really fascinating because these independent readers are expected to grade a minimum of twenty essays per hour, and they get a bonus if they hit thirty. Let's bring on the math, shall we? Thirty essays in an hour means two minutes per essay. Two minutes in which to judge one's complexity of thought, substantiality of development, and facility with language; a judgment which may very well determine whether or not somebody can even *go* to college, let alone *which* college, or the potential financial aid they might receive. The stakes in this case couldn't be higher, and to meet them, we're taught to the test, both by classroom teachers and testing teachers—'cause

FYI: specialized teachers who train kids in how to ace tests are a *Thing*. When I was in high school (and this was Michigan public school in 1993—long ago, yes, but we're not talking Laura Ingalls Wilder-one-room-schoolhouse-shit), I had a teacher who stood in front of the classroom banging a ruler on the table, and the thirty of us, in unison, would recite vocabulary words—*irony: a statement or event in which the opposite is said or the unexpected happens*—multiplied times 300 other words we'd be tested on. And yes, fine, to this day I can still recite the definition of irony, but it wasn't until years later, when I walked in on my boyfriend getting down with my roommate, that I understood what irony actually *meant*. Recitation is not learning, and tens of thousands of teenagers pulling five speed-written and panic-driven paragraphs out of their asses that will be read in two minutes by someone who can make or break their entire fucking future is no way to teach something as awesome and thoughtful and badass as the essay! I LOVE essays! I love writing them and reading them and learning from them and teaching from them, and Dear American Education System! Please stop fucking with the essay! Please stop teaching us to fear it, to speed through it, to bullshit through it. And while I'm yelling, let me be really loud and clear on this next part: *I'm talking to the system, not its teachers.* In an article at *Slate* titled "We Are Teaching High School Students to Write Terribly," Les Perelman, the retired director of MIT's Writing Across the Curriculum program, tells us that "high school teachers have to make a choice between teaching writing methods that are rewarded by SAT Essay Readers—thereby sending worse writers out into the world—or training pupils to write well generally, at the risk of parent complaints." He goes on to say that "teachers are under a huge amount of pressure to teach to the test and to get their kids high scores... they don't get a promotion, or get a lower raise. So it actually costs them to be principled. You're putting in negative incentives to be good teachers." I teach writing at the college level. At the beginning of every semester, I write the word ESSAY on the board in big letters and ask my students to share their perceptions. The word *Boring* comes up often. So does *Excruciating* and *Waste of time*. Sometimes they only have sounds: *UHG. GAH. GGRRR*. But the one that really got me, that made me want to light shit on fire and also maybe weep, was a couple of months ago when the new semester started, a student of mine said, "Essays are terrifying." "Terrifying," I said. "Why terrifying?" "Because you have to be totally, completely certain about everything," she said. "I'm eighteen years old—I'm not certain about *anything*." I tried to explain, as I always do, that an essay does not have to be definitive. It can be a place where we examine an idea, where we follow our curiosity as a way to discovery. As E.M. Forster wrote, "I don't know what I think 'til I see what I say." "That's crazy," said my student. "Nobody can pull that off in only five paragraphs."

•

In the second body paragraph of this essay about essays, I will talk about reading essays. I just read an essay by Roxane Gay that challenged me to read more diversely.[1] There's an essay by Annie Dillard that inspired me to grab life by the balls.[2] There's an essay by Kiese Layman that made dive back in to an ongoing discussion I have with myself about my own privilege.[3] There's an essay on place by Dorothy Allison that made me realize how *who* I am connects with *where* I am.[4] There's an essay by Sherman Alexie that reminded me of how a story can save us.[5] There's a whole book of essays by James Baldwin that reminds me, over and over again, of how stories are an integral part of the educational process.[6] There's an essay by Lindy West that made me feel less alone.[7] There's a whole book of essays by Samantha Irby that makes me feel less alone.[8] There's an essay by Deb Lewis that challenged me to consider what it means to be a parent.[9] There's an essay by Cheryl Strayed that gave me the permission to not have an "acceptable credit score."[10] There is an essay by Kafka, hidden in his *Diaries*—I doubt he ever would have called it an essay, but I like thinking of a writer's journal as a hundred little essays, a hundred little thoughts, one huge, messy place to make discoveries about yourself and the world. The first sentence reads:

"When I think about it, I must say that my education has done me great harm in some respects."

Then he talks about this idea for a paragraph. Then there's a space break. Then he says it again:

"When I think about it, I must say that my education has done me great harm in some respects."

He talks about it for another paragraph, coming at it from a different angle. Then:

"Often I think it over and then I always have to say that my education has done me great harm in some ways."

And he comes at it from yet another angle. This goes on seven times, each time getting deeper into the idea, and this beautiful, simple structure is something I have ripped off a thousand times, both in my essays and my own journal, as I try to slow down and figure out what I really think. Right now, in this life with its speed and its media, with my jobs and my kid, with every fucking day a challenge and a profound, crazy joy, writing is the only thing that slows me down. The only space I have to sit, quietly, and *shhhhhh. What do I think about this? How do I feel?* The structure of Kafka's piece gives me space to do that. It gives method to the madness, a road map, an option above and beyond those five paragraphs. All the essays I mentioned, any essay that you allow to teach and inspire and educate and challenge and enlighten, can give you a road map on how to write your own, how to join in this dialogue about what it means to be a human being in this crazy, mess of a world.

●

In the third body paragraph of this essay about essays I will talk about how to write essays. Read them.

●

In the final paragraph of this essay about essays, my conclusion will be... what the fuck. I don't know. In 2008, a few months after my son was born, I wrote the words *I think I need help* in my journal. I was scared I might hurt him. I didn't know there was a name for what I was feeling, that postpartum depression was a *Thing*, and that it would take three more years for me to be able to look at those words—*I need help*—without crying. When I sat down to write the piece that would eventually be selected for *The Best American Essays 2013*, there was a single question pulling me: *How do I talk about depression in a way that's not depressing?* I felt that pull throughout my entire body. It made my blood boil, was all I could talk about when I sat with my friends. In his *Letters To a Young Poet*, Rilke writes that, "a work of art is good if it has sprung from necessity." An essay is good if it has sprung from necessity. Imagine if we could teach it that way.

Footnotes:

1. Gay, Roxane. "We Are Many. We Are Everywhere." *The Rumpus.* August 3, 2012. Web.

2. Dillard, Annie. "Living Like Weasels." *Teaching a Stone To Talk.* Harper Perennial, 2013. Print.

3. Layman, Kiese. "How to Slowly Kill Yourself and Others in America." *How to Slowly Kill Yourself and Others in America.* Agate Bolden, 2013. Print.

4. Allison, Dorothy. "Place." *The Writer's Notebook.* Tin House Books, 2009. Print.

5. Alexie, Sherman. "Why The Best Kids Books Are Written in Blood." *The Wall Street Journal.* June 9, 2011. Web.

6. Baldwin, James. *Notes of a Native Son.* Beacon Press, 1984. Print.

7. West, Lindy. "Hello I Am Fat." *The Stranger.* February 11, 2011. Web.

8. Irby, Samanatha. *Meaty.* Curbside Splendor Publishing, 2013. Print.

9. Lewis, Deb. "Darkness, Then Light." *The Everyday Gay.* March 23, 2011. Web.

10. Strayed, Cheryl, "Dear Sugar: The Rumpus Advice Column #72: The Future Has An Ancient Heart." *The Rumpus.* May 5, 2011. Web.

A ROOM OF ONE'S OWN IN THE MIDDLE OF EVERYTHING

I'M WRITING ON THE BATHROOM FLOOR, laptop on my knees. It's tight in here: shower, toilet, and sink crammed together with just enough space left to stand, or in my case, sit. But even then, the door opens inwards, and you'll get whacked if you aren't careful. It's mid-afternoon, the essay I'm working on is due later tonight, this rewrite is fueled by panic, but excitement, too. I'm close. So close. I've figured out how it's supposed to go. I can hear it. Taste it. And then—

"Mommy?"

"Mommy, why is the door locked?"

"Mommy, come out, I made you a spaceship!"

Here they are: the two halves of my heart.

Until recently, I never much understood the whole *room of one's own* thing. Love me some *To The Lighthouse*, but I didn't need my own space. I could write anywhere: library, coffee shop, the bar before starting a shift. In part, I preferred writing in public—the people, the action, the white noise—but mostly, this nomadic office was determined by necessity. I lived in the city; space is expensive, and a second bedroom was a luxury I couldn't afford. Also, like many freelance artists/teachers/servers/twenty-somethings, I had three jobs—no time to spend in a second bedroom even if I had one. Also, I moved around a lot—apartment to apartment, neighborhood to neighborhood, relationship to relationship—so I learned to write whenever and wherever I could. Aren't you supposed to build your writing process around your life?

Or—wait. Is it the other way around?

I'm writing in the car, parked on a side-street, mid-Chicago winter with the heat blasting. I've got twenty precious minutes between running a faculty development workshop at one college and the fiction workshop I teach at another, and I've been writing in my head all day. Earlier, I jotted down some notes on the back of my hand; you can still see ink faded on my skin from notes the day before, and the day before that. Minutes pass and I type faster, trying to outrun them, outrun all of it, and I dread getting out of the car. Not because I dislike snow (I like it!), or the class (that, too!), but because, finally, the words are working. I can see how *this* part fits with *that* part, and I'd give my left arm for another twenty minutes.

Ten, even.

I'd take ten in a heartbeat.

It happened so fast: I fell in love, we ran away to Prague, eloped, and then returned to Chicago to resume, as they say, *real life*. It's been eight years, and still, when my husband walks into a room, I wonder what I did to get so lucky. With him, I suddenly, surprisingly, desperately wanted the whole proverbial nine yards: marriage, kids, and, inevitably, owning our own place. Right? Aren't you supposed to own your own place? Building equity? Next step towards adulthood? The American Dream and whatnot?

Thanks to a decade of working in high-end restaurants, I had a decent savings account. My husband had landed a design job that looked great on loan applications. Miraculously, neither of us carried any student debt, even with three and a half degrees between us, and we ended up being approved for a mortgage so ridiculously insane that I asked if someone had mistakenly added an extra zero. That can't be, like, *real* money! It's Monopoly money, right?

In the end, we spent less than half of our approved rate on a place we loved: a tiny, two-bedroom condo on Chicago's North Side. Nine-hundred square feet if you count the back porch. We were near public transportation, bars, and Montrose Beach. We shared an office, built bookshelves to the ceiling, and at night, would sit on the balcony listening to shows at the rock club across the street: Flaming Lips, Pixies, Yeah Yeah Yeahs. Out there, we still felt like that couple who ran away to Prague. Out there, we were young and fearless and invincible. Out there, we eased into the adults we were supposed to become.

I'm writing at Chava, a coffee shop a few blocks from home. It's Saturday, early morning, and I have until noon to take the paragraphs I've generated here and there and turn them into something cohesive, something *beginning-middle-end.* I remember how I used to write, back when nothing felt sacred and I didn't need sleep: read for a bit, write in my journal, refill coffee or wine, depending on the hour. *What music should I listen to? Does this sentence work better over here? That word isn't right, I'll get more coffee and think about it, maybe watch Buffy on FX.* It's a wonder I got anything done. Now my eye is on the clock. 8 a.m., 9 a.m., 10, 11—four precious hours until my family joins me for lunch. Afterwards, my husband will remain for his work, and our son and I take off for an adventure. Maybe we'll go to the lake, building sandcastles and screaming at seagulls. Maybe the Nature Museum, sitting as still as we can in the butterfly room. Maybe the gym, where he'll play in the KidsCenter, and I'll take a yoga class, trying to breathe into this single, quiet hour. Trying hear my own thoughts, my own heartbeat.

Like most parents, I could fill a library with stories about my kid. He's four years old now. He wants to be a superhero when he grows up. He thinks he has seven brains. He says, "Mommy, that's enough writing for today. It's time to dance!" and I close my computer and remember to live.

The day I found out I was pregnant, after the screaming and excitement and jumping up and down, I went into the tiny office I shared with my husband, squeezing past his desk to get to my own. Soon, my stomach would be too big to squeeze. Soon, this room would become the nursery. Our books and desks and equipment would go into storage—*just until we sell, of course.* Then, I'd have a new workspace, a little corner all my own.

I'm writing on the Red Line, Harrison to Lawrence, on my way home from teaching a night class. My journal is open on my lap.

I'd love to say how great it's going, how I'm so involved in the writing that I missed my L stop and had to backtrack, but that would be a lie. It's not working. Nothing's coming. I try and remember the pep talks I give my students—*Keep trying! Trust yourself! Zen and the Art of Writing!*—but fuck it. I'm too fucking tired.

Long story short: the recession hit. Four years on and off the market, and recently, we dropped our asking price to a number so ridiculously insane I asked if someone had mistakenly forgotten a zero. Eventually, we'll owe the difference to the bank, so my husband and I work to save it—six jobs now between the two of us. Four of the six we like, three of the four pay decently, two substantially.

I think of how fortunate we are to have the work.

I think of the American Dream and whatnot.

I think, again and again, of Woolf: "... a woman must have money and a room of her own."

I am writing in class while my students write. We've just had an awesome discussion about Kafka, or Gabriel Garcia Marquez, or Dorothy Allison, or Ray Bradbury, or Chimamanda Adichie, or any of a thousand writers from whom we learn our craft. My synapses are firing. I want to write, to attack my bookshelves for answers, to teach my students to attack theirs.

There are other things I'd like to teach them, as well, like the balance of writing and living. And how do you write and pay a mortgage? And is it possible to have a room of one's own without a room? But I haven't figured it out yet.

I'll always be figuring it out.

There's an envelope taped to my bathroom mirror; a reminder, if you will. It's addressed to our bank and, for now, it's empty. But when things get too hard, my husband and I talk about mailing back our keys and throwing in the towel. We've been having that conversation a lot lately; our home is one of the 11 million currently defined as "underwater," which is a poetic way of saying that we're drowning. A few weeks ago, my son asked to play Star Wars while I tried to finish an annual report for one of the jobs that pays substantially.

"Five more minutes, baby," I said, but of course, it wasn't five more minutes—it was five, five more minutes—and when I finally looked up, he was sitting on the floor holding a toy Ewok, waiting.

"Is it my turn now?" he said.

I rocked him on my lap and cried. He didn't know what was happening, and the truth is, neither did I.

Recently, I heard an accountant say, "If you want to know what you value, look at your checkbook." Mine reads like this: *Mortgage, property tax, assessments, back assessments, emergency assessments, listing fees, attorney fees.*

I'd like it to read: *Darth Vader costume, size 5T. Princess Leia buns. Plastic Light Saber, blue. Plastic Light saber, red.*

I am writing from an artist residency, all expenses paid, far away from the city in a beautiful old house. I have my own room. My own desk. Zero responsibilities save for writing and reading. It's so *still*. The sun is shining through my window. I can hear crickets. I can hear my own thoughts, , my own heartbeat. I've accomplished more in two weeks than I have in six months, and the sheer force of my gratitude could power a small city.

But.

I keep glancing up, expecting to see my kid drawing pictures at my feet. A hundred different times, I've been sure I heard him laughing in the next room. Last night, I counted mileage—*If I leave now, I could be in Chicago by bedtime. I could read him a story, wait 'til he falls asleep, and be back at the residency by midnight.*

Once again: the two halves of my heart.

I have fantasies about my future office. It doesn't need to be huge, a corner somewhere with big windows and lots of light. There will be shelves up to the ceiling with a sliding ladder— something you'd find on bookshelfporn.com. You know how some people plan for their wedding, saving pages torn from magazines of dresses and invitations and flowers? I'm planning for my room of one's own: desks and file drawers and paper-clip dispensers.

And yet I wonder: will I be able to write there? I have friends with gorgeous work spaces and all the time in the world who still write in bed, the couch, the kitchen table, the coffee shop— on the go, go, go.

It's not about the space; it's about what you do with it.

Right?

I'm writing on my back porch, three stories above Lawrence Avenue. It's late spring and warm enough to be outside but still safe from the infamous Chicago heat. Tonight is lovely in our tiny urban garden. There are popsicles made of lemonade. Asparagus on the grill. The rock club next door has its windows open for a sold-out Gotye show, and the bouncy, bass-heavy indie-pop floats in the air. Next to me, my son draws pictures of magic robots. Across from us, my husband is on his laptop, looking at art. I've just finished an essay I've been working on for weeks, arriving breathlessly at the end of the page.

Maybe this is all I need: A room of one's own in the middle of everything.

CREDITS

Many of these essays, in slightly different forms, found previous homes in literary journals and performance series. I'm grateful to those editors, producers, directors, and curators who believed in my work, and for their considerable efforts to make that work the best it could be.

"Channel B," performed for 2nd Story, published in *The Rumpus*, selected for *The Best American Essays 2013*.

"Totally Not Ethical," performed for 2nd Story, published in *Bluestem*.

"It Seems Our Time Has Run Out, Dr. Jones," performed for 2nd Story, published in *Fresh Yarn*.

"The Domino Effect," published in *Shareable*.

"Wake the Goddamn World," performed for Guts & Glory.

"The Right Kind of Water," published in *Necessary Fiction*.

"The Walls Would Be Rubble," performed for 2nd Story.

"Juggle What?" published in *Hypertext Magazine* and *The Chicago Artist Resource*.

"Who Wants the Shot," performed for 2nd Story, published in *The Good Men Project*.

"Felt Like Something," performed for 2nd Story and Listen To Your Mother, published in *f Magazine*.

"Third of Your Life," performed for 2nd Story, published in *The Way We Sleep*.

"Those Who Were There," performed for Funny Ha-Ha.

"82 Degrees," performed for 2nd Story, published in *Hypertext Magazine*.

"The OMG We've Got To Write About This Look," published in *The Nervous Breakdown*.

"We Are Fine," published in *Ms.Fit*.

"Dragons So Huge," written and performed with Bobby Biedrzycki for 2nd Story.

"NICE," performed for WRITE CLUB Chicago.

"An Essay About Essays," performed for The Paper Machete, published in *Hypertext Magazine*.

"A Room of One's Own in the Middle of Everything," published in *The Rumpus*.

ACKNOWLEDGMENTS

My profound gratitude to the team at Curbside Splendor Publishing, who threw their hearts and brains and muscle behind this book: Victor Giron, Jacob Knabb, Naomi Huffman, Ben Tanzer, and my editor, Leonard Vance, who is brilliant and, above all else, patient. Special thanks to Lauryn Allison for bringing me aboard, and to Alban Fischer, who made this thing so goddamn beautiful.

When I was a kid, my dad told me stories and my mom read books to me. They've given me many gifts over the years, but I'm most grateful for those stories and books. If I can be half the parent they are, my son is lucky indeed.

Thank you to the staff, storytellers, and audience of 2nd Story, who've inspired and challenged me for over a decade, and to the faculty, staff, and students of the Fiction Writing Department at Columbia College Chicago, where I learned—and continue to learn—the craft of writing and the art of teaching. Many thanks to the Center For Innovation in Teaching Excellence; the Ragdale Foundation; and Derrick Robles and John Latino at the Bongo Room, whose friendship and business supported me while I figured out what the hell I was doing.

All of this, the working and the writing and the running and the living—It takes a village. Lucky for me, I have one. I have the best one. Thank you, all of you, especially Randy Albers, Dia Penning, Bobby Biedrzycki, Amanda Dimond, Lott Hill, and Jeff Oaks. Again and again, you told me I could do it, and again and again, you told me I could do it better.

My whole heart is for Christopher and Caleb Jobson. In those rare moments when it's still and quiet, I shut my eyes, and think about how lucky I am, and I can't even breathe.

MEGAN STIELSTRA is the author of *Everyone Remain Calm* and the Literary Director of the 2nd Story storytelling series. She's told stories for all sorts of theaters, festivals, and bars including the Goodman, Steppenwolf, and the Museum of Contemporary Art. Her writing has appeared in *The Best American Essays, The Rumpus, The Nervous Breakdown,* and elsewhere. She teaches creative writing at Columbia College Chicago.

THE OLD NEIGHBORHOOD
A novel by Bill Hillmann

"A raucous but soulful account of growing up on the mean streets of Chicago, and the choices kids are forced to make on a daily basis. This cool, incendiary rites of passage novel is the real deal."
—Irvine Welsh, *author of* Trainspotting

A bright and sensitive teen, Joe Walsh is the youngest in a big, mixed-race Chicago family. After Joe witnesses his heroin-addicted oldest brother commit a brutal gangland murder, his friends and loved ones systematically drag him deeper into a black pit of violence that reaches a bloody impasse when his eldest sister begins dating a rival gang member.

MEATY Essays by Samantha Irby

"Blunt, sharp and occasionally heartbreaking, Samantha Irby's Meaty *marks the arrival of a truly original voice. You don't need difficult circumstances to become a great writer, but you need a great writer to capture life's weird turns with such honesty and wit."*

—John August, *acclaimed screenwriter and filmmaker*

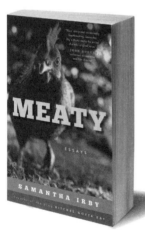

Samantha Irby explodes onto the page in her debut collection of brand-new essays about being a complete dummy trying to laugh her way through her ridiculous life of failed relationships, taco feasts, bouts with Crohn's Disease, and more, all told with the same scathing wit and poignant candor long-time readers have come to expect from her notoriously hilarious blog, bitchesgottaeat.com.